MANIFESTO ROSAE CRUCIS

MANIFESTO ROSAE CRUCIS

CONTENTS

FAMA FRATERNITATIS

or a Discovery of the Fraternity of the Most Laudable Order of the Rosy Cross

CONFESSIO FRATERNITATIS

The Confession of the Laudable Fraternity of the Most Honorable Order of the Rosy Cross, Written to All the Learned of Europe

THE CHEMICAL WEDDING OF CHRISTIAN ROSENKRUETZ

MANIFESTO ROSAE CRUCIS

"We, the Deputies of the Higher College of the Rose-Croix, do make our stay, visibly and invisibly, in this city, by the grace of the Most High, to Whom turn the hearts of the Just. We demonstrate and instruct, without books and distinctions, the ability to speak all manners of tongues of the countries where we choose to be, in order to draw our fellow creatures from error of death. "He who takes it upon himself to see us merely out of curiosity will never make contact with us. But if his inclination seriously impels him to register in our fellowship, we, who are judges of intentions, will cause him to see the truth of our promises; to the extent that we shall not make known the place of our meeting in this city, since the thoughts attached to the real desire of the seeker will lead us to him and him to us."

FAMA FRATERNITATIS

OR A DISCOVERY OF THE FRATERNITY OF THE MOST LAUDABLE ORDER OF THE ROSY CROSS

Seeing the only wise and merciful God in these latter days hath poured out so richly his mercy and goodness to mankind, where by we do attain more and more to the perfect knowledge of his Son Jesus Christ and Nature, that justly we may boast of the happy time, wherein there is not only discovered unto us the half part of the world, which was heretofore unknown and hidden, but he hath also made manifest unto us many wonderful, and never heretofore seen, works and creatures of Nature, and moreover hath raised men, imbued with great wisdom, who might partly renew and reduce all arts (in this our age spotted and imperfect) to perfection; so that finally man might thereby understand his own nobleness and worth, and why he is called Microcosmus *(the lesser universe)*, and how far his knowledge extendeth into Nature.

Although the rude world herewith will he but little pleased, but rather smile and scoff thereat; also the pride and covetousness of the learned is so great, it will not suffer them to agree together; but were they united, they might out of all those things which in this our age God doth so richly bestow upon us, collect *Librum Naturae*, or a perfect method of all arts: but such is their opposition, that they still keep, and are loth to leave the old course, esteeming *Porphyry (Popery)*, *Aristotle*, and *Galen*, yea and that which bath but a mere show of learning, more than the clear and manifested light and truth; who if they were now living, with much joy would leave their erroneous doctrines. But here is too great weakness for such a great work. And although in theology, physics, and the mathematics, the truth doth oppose itself (the truth doth manifest itself) nevertheless the old enemy by his subtlety and craft doth show himself in hindering every good purpose by his instruments and contentious wavering people. To such an intent of a general reformation, the most godly and highly illuminated father, our brother, C.R. a German, the chief and original of our Fraternity, hath much and long time laboured, who by reason of his poverty (although descended of noble parents) in the fifth year of his age was placed in a cloister, where he had learned indifferently the Greek and Latin tongues, who (upon his earnest desire and request) being yet in his growing years, was associated to a brother, P.A.L. who had determined to go to the Holy Land.

Although this brother died in Ciprus (Cyprus), and so never came to Jerusalem, yet our brother C.R. did not return, but shipped himself over, and went to Damasco (Damascus), minding from thence to go to Jerusalem; but by reason of the feebleness of his body he remained still there, and by his skill in physic he obtained much favour with the Turks. In the meantime he became by chance acquainted with the wise men of Damasco in Arabia, and beheld what great wonders they wrought, and how Nature was discovered unto them; hereby was that high and noble spirit of brother C.R. so stirred up, that Jerusalem was not so much now in his mind as Damasco; also he could not bridle his desires any longer, but made a bargain with the Arabians, that they should carry him for a certain sum of money to Damasco; he was but of the age of sixteen years when he came thither, yet of a strong Dutch constitution. There the wise received him (as he himself witnesseth) not as a stranger, but as one whom they had long expected; they called him by his name, and showed him other secrets out of his cloister, whereat he could not but mightily wonder. He learned there better the Arabian tongue, so that the year following he translated the book M. into good Latin, which he afterwards brought with him. This is the place where he did learn his physicks, and his mathematicks, whereof the world hath just cause to rejoice, if there were more love, and less envy. After three years he returned again with good consent, shipped himself over *Sinus Arabicus* into Egypt, where he remained not long, but only took better notice there of the plants and creatures. He sailed over the whole Mediterranean sea for to come unto Fez, where the Arabians had directed him. And it is a great shame unto us, that wise men, so far remote the one from the other, should not only be of one opinion, hating all contentious writings, but also be so willing and ready under the seal of secrecy to impart their secrets to others.

Every year the Arabians and Africans do send one to another, inquiring one of another out of their arts, if happily they had found out some better things, or if experience had weakened their reasons. Yearly there came something to light, whereby the mathematica, physic, and magic (for in those are they of Fez most skilful) were amended. As there is nowadays in Germany no want of learned men, *magicians, cabalists, physicians,* and *philosophers,* were there but more love and kindness among them, or that the most part of them would not keep their secrets close only to themselves. At Fez he did get acquaintance with those which are commonly called the Elementary Inhabitants, who revealed unto him many of their secrets. As we Germans likewise might gather together many things, if there were the like unity, and desire of searching out secrets amongst us.

Of these of Fez he often did confess that their *Magia* was not altogether pure, and also that their *Cabala* was defiled with their religion; but notwithstanding he knew how to make good use of the same, and found still more better grounds for his faith, altogether agreeable with the harmony of the whole world, and wonderfully impressed in all periods of times. And thence proceedeth that fair concord, that, as in every several kernel is contained a whole good tree or fruit, so likewise is included in the little body of man the whole great world, whose religion, policy, health, members, nature, language, words and works, are agreeing, sympathizing, and in equal tune and melody with God, heaven, and earth. And that which is dis-agreeing with them is error, falsehood, and of the Devil, who alone is the first, middle, and last cause of strife, blindness, and darkness in the world. Also, might one examine all and several persons upon the earth, he should find that which is good and right, is always agreeing with itself; but all the rest is spotted with a thousand erroneous conceits.

After two years brother C.R. departed the city of Fez, and sailed with many costly things into Spain, hoping well [that since] he himself had so well and so profitably spent his time in his travel, that the learned in Europe would highly rejoice with him, and begin to rule and order all their studies according to those sound and sure foundations. He therefore conferred with the learned in Spain, showing unto them the errors of our arts, and how they might be corrected, and from whence they should gather the true *Indicia* of the times to come, and wherein they ought to agree with those things that are past; also how the faults of the Church and the whole *Philosophia Moralis* was to be amended. He showed them new growths, new fruits, and beasts, which did concord with old philosophy, and prescribed them new *Axiomata*, whereby all things might fully be restored. But it was to them a laughing matter; and being a new thing unto them, they feared that their great name should be lessened, if they should now again begin to learn and acknowledge their many years errors, to which they were accustomed, and wherewith with they had gained them enough. Who-so loveth unquietness, let him be reformed.

The same song was also sung to him by other nations, the which moved him the more because it happened to him contrary to his expectations, being ready then bountifully to impart all his arts and secrets to the learned, if they would have but undertaken to write the true and infallible *Axiomata*, out of all faculties, sciences, and arts, and whole Nature, as that which he knew would direct them, like a globe or circle, to the only middle point and *Centrum*, and (as is usual among the Arabians) it should only serve to the wise and learned as a rule. That also there might be a Society in Europe, which might have gold, silver, and precious stones, sufficient for to bestow them on kings, for their necessary uses and lawful purposes; with which such as be governors might be brought up, for to learn all that which God hath suffered man to know, and thereby to he enabled in all times of need to give their counsel unto those that seek it, like the heathen oracles. Verily we must confess that the world in those days was already big with those great commotions, labouring to be delivered of them; and did bring forth painful, worthy men, who broke with all force through darkness and barbarism, and left us who succeeded to follow them: and assuredly they have been the uppermost point in *trigono igneo*, whose flame now should be more and more bright, and shall undoubtedly give to the world the last light.

Such a one likewise hath Theophrastus been in vocation and callings, although he was none of our Fraternity, yet nevertheless hath he diligently read over the book M: whereby his sharp *ingenium* was exalted; but this man was also hindered in his course by the multitude of the learned and wise-seeming men, that he was never able peacefully to confer with others of his knowledge and understanding he had of Nature. And therefore in his writing he rather mocked these busy bodies, and doth not show them altogether what he was: yet nevertheless there is found with him well grounded the aforenamed *Harmonia*, which without doubt he had imparted to the learned, if he had not found them rather worthy of subtle vexation, than to be instructed in greater arts and sciences; he then with a free and careless life lost his time, and left unto the world their foolish pleasures.

But that we do not forget our loving father, brother C.R., he after many painful travels, and his fruitless true instructions, returned again into Germany, the which he (by reason of the alterations which were shortly to come, and of the strange and dangerous contentions) heartily loved. There, although he could have bragged with his art, but specially of the transmutations of metals, yet did he esteem more Heaven, and the citizens thereof, Man, than all vain glory and pomp.

Nevertheless he built a fitting and neat habitation, in which he ruminated his voyage, and philosophy, and reduced them together in a true memorial. In this house he spent a great time in the mathematicks, and made many fine instruments, *ex omnibus hajus artis partibus*, whereof there is but little remaining to us, as hereafter you shall understand. After five years came again into his mind the wished for reformation; and in regard he doubted of the aid and help of others, although he himself was painful, lusty, and unwearying, he undertook, with some few joined with him, to attempt the same. Wherefore he desired to this end, to have out of his first cloister (to the which he bare a great affection) three of his brethren, brother G.V., brother J.A., and brother J.O., who besides that, they had some more knowledge in the arts, than in that time many others had, he did bind those three unto himself, to be faithful, diligent, and secret; as also to commit carefully to writing, all that which he should direct and instruct them in, to the end that those which were to come, and through especial revelation should be received into this Fraternity, might not be deceived of the least syllable and word.

After this manner began the Fraternity of the *Rose Cross*; first, by four persons only, and by them was made the magical language and writing, with a large dictionary, which we yet daily use to God's praise and glory, and do find great wisdom therein; they made also the first part of the book M. But in respect that that labour was too heavy, and the unspeakable concourse of the sick hindered them, and also whilst his new building (called *Sancti spiritus*) was now finished, they concluded to draw and receive yet others more into their Fraternity; to this end was chosen brother R.C., his deceased father's brother's son, brother B. a skilful painter, G. and P.D. their secretary, all Germans except J.A. so in all they were eight in number, all bachelors and of vowed virginity; by those was collected a book or volume of all that which man can desire, wish, or hope for.

Although we do now freely confess, that the world is much amended within an hundred years, yet we are assured that our *Axiomata* shall unmovably remain unto the world's end, and also the world in her highest and last age shall not attain to see anything else; for our *Rota* takes her beginning from that day when God spake *Fiat*, and shall end when he shall speak *Pereat*; yet God's clock striketh every minute, where ours scarce striketh perfect hours. We also steadfastly believe, that if our brethren and fathers had lived in this our present and clear light, they would more roughly have handled the Pope, Mahomet, scribes, artists, and sophisters, and had showed themselves more helpful, not simply with sighs, and wishing of their end and consummation.

When now these eight brethren had disposed and ordered all things in such manner, as there was not now need of any great labour, and also that everyone was sufficiently instructed, and able perfectly to discourse of secret and manifest philosophy, they would not remain any longer together, but as in the beginning they had agreed, they separated themselves into several countries, because that not only their *Axiomata* might in secret be more profoundly examined by the learned, but that they themselves, if in some country or other they observed anything, or perceived some error, they might inform one another of it.

Their agreement was this: First, That none of them should profess any other thing than to cure the sick, and that *gratis*. 2. None of the posterity should be constrained to wear one certain kind of habit, but therein to follow the custom of the country. 3. That every year upon the day C. they should meet together in the house *S. Spiritus*, or write the cause of his absence. 4. Every brother should look about for a worthy person, who, after his decease, might succeed him. 5. The word C.R. should be their seal, mark, and character. 6. The Fraternity should remain secret one hundred years. These six articles they bound themselves one to another to keep, and five of the brethren departed, only the brethren B. and D. remained with the father, Fra. R. C., a whole year; when these likewise departed. Then remained by him his cousin and brother J.O. so that he hath all the days of his life with him two of his brethren. And although that as yet the Church was not cleansed, nevertheless we know that they did think of her, and what with longing desire they looked for. Every year they assembled together with joy, and made a full resolution of that which they had done; there must certainly have been great pleasure, to hear truly and without invention related and rehearsed all the wonders which God had poured out here and there through the world. Everyone may hold it out for certain, that such persons as were sent, and joined together by God, and the heavens, and chosen out of the wisest of men, as have lived in many ages, did live together above all others in highest unity, greatest secrecy, and most kindness one towards another.

After such a most laudable sort they did spend their lives, and although they were free from all diseases and pain, yet notwithstanding they could not live and pass their time appointed of God. The first of this Fraternity which died, and that in England, was J.O., as brother C. long before had foretold him; he was very expert, and well learned in *Cabala*, as his book called H. witnesseth. In England he is much spoken of; and chiefly because he cured a young Earl of Norfolk of the leprosy. They had concluded, that as much as possibly could be, their burial place should be kept secret, as at this day it is not known unto us what is become of some of them, yet everyone's place was supplied with a fit successor. But this we will confess publicly by these presents to the honour of God, that what secrets soever we have learned out of the book M. (although before our eyes we behold the image and pattern of all the world) yet are there not shown unto us our misfortunes, nor hour of death, the which only is known to God himself, who thereby would have us keep in a continual readiness. But hereof more in our Confession, where we do set down 37 reasons wherefore we now do make known our Fraternity, and proffer such high mysteries, and without constraint and reward. Also we do promise more gold than both the Indies bring to the King of Spain; for Europe is with child and will bring forth a strong child, who shall stand in need of a great godfather's gift.

After the death of J.O., brother R.C. rested not, but as soon as he could, called the rest together (and as we suppose) then his grave was made. Although hitherto we (who were the latest) did not know when our loving father R.C. died, and had no more but the bare names of the beginners, and all their successors, to us, yet there came into our memory a secret, which through dark and hidden words, and speeches of the 100 years, brother A., the successor of D. (who was of the last and second row and succession, and had lived amongst many of us) did impart unto us of the third row and succession. Otherwise we must confess, that after the death of the said A. none of us had in any manner known anything of brother R.C. and of his first fellow-brethren, than that which was extant of them in our philosophical *Bibliotheca*, amongst which our *Axiomata* was held for the chiefest, *Rota Mundi* for the most artificial, and *Protheus* the most profitable. Likewise we do not certainly know if these of the second row have been of the like wisdom as the first, and if they were admitted to all things. It shall be declared hereafter to the gentle Reader, not only what we have heard of the burial of R.C., but also made manifest publicly by the foresight, sufferance, and commandment of God, whom we most faithfully obey, that if we shall be answered discreetly and Christian-like, we will not be afraid to set forth publicly in print our names and surnames, our meetings, or anything else that may be required at our hands.

Now the true and fundamental relation of the finding out of the high illuminated man of God, Fra. C.R.C. is this. After that A. in *Gallia Narbonensis* was deceased, then succeeded in his place our loving brother N.N. This man after he had repaired unto us to take the solemn oath of fidelity and secrecy, he informed us *bona fide,* that A. had comforted him in telling him that this Fraternity should ere long not remain so hidden, but should be to all the whole German nation helpful, needful, and commendable; of the which he was not in any wise in his estate ashamed of. The year following, after he had performed his school right and was minded now to travel, being for that purpose sufficiently provided with Fortunatus' purse, he thought (he being a good architect) to alter something of his building and to make it more fit. In such renewing he lighted upon the memorial table which was cast of brass, and containeth all the names of the brethren, with some few other things. This he would transfer in another more fitting vault; for where or when Fra R.C. died, or in what country he was buried, was by our predecessors concealed and unknown to us. In this table stuck a great nail somewhat strong, so that when he was with force drawn out, he took with him an indifferently big stone out of the thin wall, or plastering, of the hidden door, and so, unlooked for, uncovered the door. wherefore we did with by and longing throw down the rest of the wall, and cleared the door) upon which was written in great letters, *Post 120 annos patebo* (after 120 years I shall open.), with the year of the Lord under it. Therefore we gave God thanks and let it rest that same night, because we would first overlook our *Rotam*. But we refer ourselves again to the Confession, for what we here publish is done for the help of those that are worthy, but to the unworthy (God willing) it will he small profit. For like as our door was after so many years wonderfully discovered, also there shall be opened a door to Europe (when the wall is removed) which already doth begin to appear, and with great desire is expected of many.

In the morning following we opened the door, and there appeared to our sight a vault of seven sides and corners, every side five foot broad, and the height of eight foot. Although the sun never shined in this vault, nevertheless it was enlightened with another sun, which had learned this from the sun, and was situated in the upper part in the center of the ceiling. In the midst, instead of a tombstone, was a round altar covered over with a plate of brass, and thereon this engraven:

A.C.R.C. Hoc universi compendium vivus mihi sepulchrum feci (This compendium of the Universe I have made in my lifetime to be my tomb)

Round about the first circle, or brim, stood, *Jesus mihi omnia* (Jesus is all things to me)

In the middle were four figures, inclosed in circles, whose circumscription was,

1. *Nequaquam vacuum* (A Vacuum exists nowhere.)

2. *Legis Jugum* (The Yoke of the Law)

3. *Libertas Evangelii* (the Liberty of the Gospel)

4. *Dei gloria intacta* (The Whole Glory of God)

This is all clear and bright; as also the seven sides and the two *Heptagoni*: so we kneeled altogether down, and gave thanks to the sole wise, sole mighty and sole eternal God, who hath taught us more than all men's wits could have found out, praised be his holy name. This vault we parted in three parts, the upper part or ceiling, the wall or side, the ground or floor.

Of the upper part you shall understand no more of it at this time, but that it was divided according to the seven sides in the triangle, which was in the bright center; but what therein is contained, you shall God willing (that are desirous of our society) behold the same with your own eyes; but every side or wall is parted into ten figures, every one with their several figures and sentences, as they are truly shown and set forth *Concentratum* here in our book.

The bottom again is parted in the triangle, but because therein is described the power and the rule of the inferior governors, we leave to manifest the same, for fear of the abuse by the evil and ungodly world. But those that are provided and stored with the heavenly antidote, they do without fear or hurt tread on and bruise the head of the old and evil serpent, which this our age is well fitted for. Every side or wall had a door or chest, wherein there lay divers things, especially all our books, which otherwise we had. Besides the *Vocabular* of *Theoph: Par. Ho.*(Theophrasti Paracelsi ab Hohenheim, or Paracelsus) and these which daily unfalsifieth we do participate. Herein also we found his *Itinerarium* and *vitam*, whence this relation for the most part is taken. In another chest were looking-glasses of divers virtues, as also in another place were little bells, burning lamps, and chiefly wonderful artificial songs, generally all done to that end, that if it should happen after many hundred years the Order or Fraternity should come to nothing, they might by this only vault be restored again.

Now as yet we had not seen the dead body of our careful and wise father, we therefore removed the altar aside, there we lifted up a strong plate of brass, and found a fair and worthy body, whole and unconsumed, as the same is here lively counterfeited, with all his ornaments and attires. In his hand he held a parchment book, called I., the which next unto the Bible is our greatest treasure, which ought to be delivered to the censure of the world. At the end of this book standeth this following Elogium:

Granum pectori Jesu insitum.

C. Ros. C. ex nobili atque splendida Germaniae R.C. familia oriundus, vir sui seculi divinis revelatiombus subtilissimis imaginationibus, indefessis laboribus ad coetestia, atque humana mysteria; arcanave admissus postquam suam (quam Arabico, & Africano itineribus Collegerat) plusquam regiam, atque imperatoriam Gazam suo seculo nondum convenientem, posteritati eruendam custodivisset & jam suarum Artium, ut & nominis, fides acconjunctissimos herides instituisset, mundum minitum omnibus motibus magno illi respondentem fabricasset hocque tandem preteritarum, praesentium, & futurarum, rerum compendio extracto, centenario major non morbo (quem ipse nunquam corpore expertus erat, nunquam alios infestare sinebat) ullo pellente sed spiritu Dei evocante, illuminatam animam (inter Fratrum amplexus & ultima oscula) fidelissimo creatori Deo reddidisset, Pater dilectissimus, Fra: suavissimus, praeceptor fidelissimus, amicus integerimus, a suis ad 120 annos hic absconditus est." (A grain buried in the breast of Jesus. C. Ros. C., sprung from the noble and renowned German family of R.C.: a man admitted into the mysteries and secrets of heaven and earth through the divine revelations, subtle cognitions and unwearied toil of his life. In his journeys through Arabia and Africa he collected a treasure surpassing that of Kings and Emperors; but finding it not suitable for his times, he kept it guarded for posterity to uncover, and appointed loyal and faithful heirs of his arts and also of his name. He constructed a microcosm corresponding in all motions to the macrocosm and finally drew up this compendium of things past, present and to come. Then, having now passed the century of years, though oppressed by no disease, which he had neither felt in his own body nor allowed to attack others, but summoned by the Spirit of God, amid the last embraces of his brethren he rendered up his illuminated soul to God his Creator. A beloved Father, an affectionate Brother, a faithful Teacher, a loyal Friend. He was hidden by his disciples for 120 years.)

Underneath they had subscribed themselves,

1. *Fra. I.A., Fr. C.H. electione Fraternitatis caput.* (by the choice of Fra. C.H., head of the fraternity.)

2. *Fr. G.V. M.P.C.*

3. *Fra. R.C. Iunior haeres S. Spiritus*

4. *Fra. B.M., P.A. Pictor & Architectus*

5. *Fr. C.G. M.P.I. Cabalista*

Secundi Circuli

1. Fra. P.A. Successor, Fr. I.O. Mathematicus

2. Fra. A. Successor Fra. P.D. 3. Fra. R. Successor patris C.R.C. cum Christo triumphant.

At the end was written

Ex Deo nascimur, in Jesu morimur, per spiritum sanctum revivscimus (We are born from God, we die in Jesus, we live again though the Holy Spirit.)

At that time was already dead brother I.O. and Fra. D. but their burial place where is it to be found? We doubt not but our Fra. Senior hath the same, and some especial thing laid in earth, and perhaps likewise hidden. We also hope that this our example will stir up others more diligently to inquire after their names (whom we have therefore published) and to search for the place of their burial; for the most part of them, by reason of their practise and physic, are yet known, and praised among very old folks; so might perhaps our Gaza be enlarged, or at least be better cleared.

Concerning *Minutum Mundum*, we found it kept in another little altar, truly more fine than can be imagined by any understanding man; but we will leave him undescribed, until we shall truly be answered upon this our true hearted *Fama*. And so we have covered it again with the plates, and set the altar thereon, shut the door, and made it sure, with all our seals. Besides by instruction and command of our *Rota*, there are come to sight some books, among which is contained M. (which were made instead of household care by the praiseworthy M.P.). Finally we departed the one from the other, and left the natural heirs in possession of our jewels. And so we do expect the answer and judgment of the learned, or unlearned.

Howbeit we know after a time there will now be a general reformation, both of divine and human things, according to our desire, and the expectation of others. For it is fitting, that before the rising of the sun, there should appear and break forth *Aurora*, or some clearness, or divine light in the sky. And so in the mean time some few, who shall give their names, may join together, thereby to increase the number and respect of our Fraternity, and make a happy and wished for beginning of our *Philosophical Canons*, prescribed to us by our brother R.C., and be partakers with us of our treasures (which never can fail or be wasted), in all humility and love to be eased of this world's labour, and not walk so blindly in the knowledge of the wonder-fill works of God.

But that also every Christian may know of what religion and belief we are, we confess to have the knowledge of Jesus Christ (as the same now in these last days, and chiefly in Germany, most clear and pure is professed, and is nowadays cleansed and void of all swerving people, heretics, and false prophets), in certain noted countries maintained, defended and propagated. Also we use two Sacraments, as they are instituted with all forms and ceremonies of the first reformed Church. In *Politia* we acknowledge the Roman Empire and *Quartam Monarchiam* for our Christian head; albeit we know what alterations be at hand, and would fain impart the same with all our hearts to other godly learned men; notwithstanding our hand-writing which is in our hands, no man (except God alone) can make it common, nor any unworthy person is able to bereave us of it. But we shall help with secret aid this so good a cause, as God shall permit or hinder us. For our God is not blind, as the heathen Fortuna, but is the Church's ornament, and the honour of the Temple. Our Philosophy also is not a new invention, but as *Adam* after his fall hath received it) and as *Moses* and *Solomon* used it. Also she ought not much to be doubted of; or contradicted by other opinions, or meanings; but seeing the truth is peaceable, brief; and always like herself in all things, and especially accorded by with *Jesus in omni parte* and all members. And as he is the true Image of the Father, so is she his Image. It shall not be said, this is true according to *Philosophy*, but true according to *Theologie*. And wherein *Plato, Aristotle, Pythagoras* and others did hit the mark, and wherein *Enoch, Abraham, Moses, Solomon* did excel, but especially wherewith that wonderful book the Bible agreeth. All that same concurreth together, and makes a sphere or Globe, whose total parts are equidistant from the Centre, as hereof more at large and more plain shall be spoken of in Christianly conference.

But now concerning (and chiefly in this our age) the ungodly and accursed *gold-making*, which hath gotten so much the upper hand, whereby under colour of it, many runagates and roguish people do use great villanies and cozen and abuse the credit which is given them. Yea nowadays men of discretion do hold the transmutation of metals to be the highest point and *fastigium* in *philosophy*, this is all their intent and desire, and that God would be most esteemed by them, and honoured, which could make great store of gold, and in abundance, the which with unpremeditate prayers, they hope to attain of the all-knowing God, and searcher of all hearts. We therefore do by these presents publicly testify, that the true philosophers are far of another mind, esteeming little the making of gold, which is but a *parergon*; for besides that they have a thousand better things.

And we say with our loving father R.C.C. *Phy: aurum nisi quantum: aurum,* for unto them the whole nature is detected: he doth not rejoice that he can make gold, and that, as saith Christ, the devils are obedient unto him; but is glad that he seeth the heavens open, and the angels of God ascending and descending, and his name written in the book of life. Also we do testify that under the name of *Chymia* many books and pictures are set forth in *Contumeliam gloriae Dei,* as we will name them in their due season, and will give to the pure-hearted a Catalogue, or register of them. And we pray all learned men to take heed of these kind of books; for the enemy never resteth but soweth his weeds, till a stronger one doth root it out. So according to the will and meaning of *Fra C.R.C.* we his brethren request again all the learned in Europe who shall read (sent forth in five languages) this our *Famam* and *Confessionem,* that it would please them with good deliberation to ponder this our offer, and to examine most nearly and most sharply their arts, and behold the present time with all diligence, and to declare their mind, either *Communicatio consilio,* or *singulatim* by print.And although at this time we make no mention either of names or meetings, yet nevertheless everyone's opinion shall assuredly come to our hands, in what language so ever it be; nor anybody shall fail, who so gives his name, but to speak with some of us, either by word of mouth, or else, if there be some let, in writing. And this we say for a truth, that whosoever shall earnestly, and from his heart, bear affection unto us, it shall be beneficial to him in goods, body, and soul; but he that is false-hearted, or only greedy of riches, the same first of all shall not be able in any manner of wise to hurt us, but bring himself to utter ruin and destruction. Also our building (although one hundred thousand people had very near seen and beheld the same) shall for ever remain untouched, undestroyed, and hidden to the wicked world.

SUB UMBRA ALARUM TUARUM JEHOVA (Under the shadow of thy wings, Jehovah).

CONFESSIO FRATERNITATIS

THE CONFESSION OF THE LAUDABLE FRATERNITY OF THE MOST HONORABLE ORDER OF THE ROSY CROSS, WRITTEN TO ALL THE LEARNED OF EUROPE.

Whatsoever is published, and made known to everyone, concerning our Fraternity, by the foresaid *Fama*, let no man esteem lightly of it, nor hold it as an idle or invented thing, and much less receive the same, as though it were only a mere conceit of ours. It is the Lord Jehovah (who seeing the Lord's Sabbath is almost at hand, and hastened again, his period or course being finished, to his first beginning) doth turn about the course of Nature; and what heretofore hath been sought with great pains, and daily labour, is now manifested unto those who make small account, or scarcely once think upon it; but those which desire it, it is in a manner forced and thrust upon them, that thereby the life of the godly may be eased of all their toil and labour, and be no more subject to the storms of inconstant Fortune; but the wickedness of the ungodly thereby, with their due and deserved punishment, be augmented and multiplied.

Although we cannot be by any suspected of the least heresy, or of any wicked beginning, or purpose against the worldly government, we do condemn the East and the West (meaning the Pope and Mahomet) blasphemers against our Lord Jesus Christ, and offer and present with a good will to the chief head of the Roman Empire our prayers, secrets, and great treasures of gold.

Yet we have thought good, and fit for the learned's sakes, to add somewhat more to this, and make a better explanation if there be anything too deep, hidden, and set down over dark in the *Fama*, or for certain reasons were altogether omitted, and left out; hoping herewith the learned will be more addicted unto us, and be made far more fit and willing for our purpose.

Concerning the alteration and amendment of Philosophy, we have (as much as at this present is needful) sufficiently declared, to wit, that the same is altogether weak and faulty; yet we doubt not, although the most part falsely do allege that she (I know not how) is sound and strong, yet notwithstanding she fetches her last breath and is departing.

But as commonly, even in the same place or country where there breaketh forth a new and unaccustomed disease, Nature also there discovereth a medicine against the same; so there doth appear for so manifold infirmities of Philosophy the right means, and unto our Patria sufficiently offered, whereby she may become sound again, which is now to be renewed and altogether new.

No other Philosophy we have, than that which is the head and sum, the foundations and contents of all faculties, sciences, and arts, the which (if we well behold our age) containeth much of Theology and medicine, but little of the wisdom of the law, and doth diligently search both heaven and earth: or, to speak briefly thereof; which doth manifest and declare sufficiently Man, whereof all learned who will make themselves known unto us, and come into our brotherhood, shall find more wonderful secrets by us than heretofore they did attain unto, and did know, or are able to believe or utter.

Wherefore, to declare briefly our meaning hereof, we ought to labour carefully that there be not only a wondering at our meeting and adhortation, but that likewise everyone may know, that although we do not lightly esteem and regard such mysteries and secrets, we nevertheless hold it fit, that the knowledge thereof be manifested and revealed to many.

For it is to be taught and believed, that this our unhoped [for], willing offer will raise many and divers thoughts in men, unto whom (as yet) be unknown *Miranda sexta aetatis*, or those which by reason of the course of the world, esteem the things to come like unto the present, and are hindered through all manner of importunities of this our time, so that they live no otherwise in the world, than blind fools, who can, in the clear sunshine day discern and know nothing, than only by feeling.

Now concerning the first part, we hold this, that the mediations, knowledge and inventions of our loving Christian Father (of all that, which from the beginning of the world, Man's wisdom, either through God's revelation, or through the service of the angels and spirits, or through the sharpness and depth of understanding, or through long observation, use, and experience, bath found out, invented, brought forth, corrected, and till now bath been propagated and transplanted) are so excellent, worthy and great, that if all books should perish, and by God's almighty sufferance, all writings and all learnings should be lost, yet the posterity will be able only thereby to lay a new foundation, and bring truth to light again; the which perhaps would not be so hard to do as if one should begin to pull down and destroy the old ruinous building, and then to enlarge the fore court, afterwards bring lights in the lodgings, and then change the doors, stair, and other things according to our intention.

But to whom would not this be acceptable, for to be manifested to everyone rather than to have it kept and spared, as an especial ornament for the appointed time to come?

Wherefore should we not with all our hearts rest and remain in the only truth (which men through so many erroneous and crooked ways do seek) if it had only pleased God to lighten unto us the sixth *Candelabrium*? Were it not good that we needed not to care, not to fear hunger, poverty, sickness and age?

Were it not a precious thing, that you could always live so, as if you had lived from the beginning of the world, and, moreover, as you should still live to the end thereof? Were it not excellent you dwell in one place, that neither the people which dwell beyond the River Ganges in the Indies could hide anything, nor those which live in Peru might be able to keep secret their counsels from thee?

Were it not a precious thing, that you could so read in one only book, and withal by reading understand and remember, all that which in all other books (which heretofore have been, and are now, and hereafter shall come out) hath been, is, and shall he learned and found out of them?

How pleasant were it, that you could so sing, that instead of stony rocks you could draw the pearls and precious stones, instead of wild beasts, spirits, and instead of hellish Pluto, move the mighty princes of the world.

O ye people, God's counsel is far otherwise, who hath concluded now to increase and enlarge the number of our Fraternity, the which we with such joy have undertaken, as we have heretofore obtained this great treasure without our merits, yea without our hopes, and thoughts, and purpose with the like fidelity to put the same in practise, that neither the compassion nor pity of our own children (which some of us in the Fraternity have) shall draw us from it, because we know these unhoped for goods cannot be inherited, nor by chance be obtained.

If there be some body now, which on the other side will complain of our discretion, that we offer our treasures so freely, and without any difference to all men, and do not rather regard and respect more the godly, learned, wise, or princely persons, than the common people; those we do not contradict, seeing it is not a slight and easy matter; but withal we signify so much, that our *Arcana* or secrets will no ways be common, and generally made known. Although the *Fama* be set forth in five languages, and is manifested to everyone, yet we do partly very well know that the unlearned and gross wits will not receive nor regard the same; as also the worthiness of those who shall be accepted into our Fraternity are not esteemed and known of us by Man's carefulness, but by the Rule of our Revelation and Manifestation. Wherefore if the unworthy cry and call a thousand times, or if they shall offer and present themselves to us a thousand times, yea God hath commanded our ears, that they should hear none of them: yea God hath so compassed us about with his clouds, that unto us his servants no violence or force can be done or committed; wherefore we neither can be seen or known by anybody, except he had the eyes of an eagle. It hath been necessary that the *Fama* should be set forth in everyone's mother tongue, because those should not be defrauded of the knowledge thereof, whom (although they be unlearned) God hath not excluded from the happiness of this Fraternity, the which shall be divided and parted into certain degrees; as those which dwell in the city of Damcar (Damascus) in Arabia, who have a far different politick order from the other Arabians. For there do govern only wise and understanding men, who by the king's permission make particular laws; according unto which example also the government shall be instituted in Europe (whereof we have a description set down by our Christianly Father) when first is done and come to pass that which is to precede. And thenceforth our Trumpet shall publicly sound with a loud sound, and great noise, when namely the same (which at this present is shown by few, and is secretly, as a thing to come, declared in figures and pictures) shall be free and publicly proclaimed, and the whole world shall be filled withal. Even in such manner as heretofore, many godly people have secretly and altogether desperately pushed at the Pope's tyranny, which afterwards, with great, earnest, and especial zeal in Germany, was thrown from his seat, and trodden underfoot, whose final fall is delayed, and kept for our times, when he also shall be scratched in pieces with nails, and an end be made of his ass's cry, by a new voice; The which we know is already reasonably manifest and known to many learned men in Germany, as their writings and secret congratulations do sufficiently witness the same.

We could here relate and declare what all the time, from the year of Our Lord 1378 (in which year our Christian Father was born) till now, hath happened, where we might rehearse what alterations he hath seen in the world these one hundred and six years of his life, which he hath left to our brethren and us after his decease to peruse. But brevity, which we do observe, will not permit at this present to make rehearsal of it, till a more fit time. At this time it is enough for those which do not despise our declaration, haying therefore briefly touched it, thereby to prepare the way for their acquaintance and friendship with us.

Yet to whom it is permitted that he may see, and for his instruction use, those great letters and characters which the Lord God hath written and imprinted in heaven and earth's edifice, through the alteration of government, which hath been from time to time altered and renewed, the same is already (although as yet unknown to himself) ours. And as we know he will not despise our inviting and calling, so none shall fear any deceit, for we promise and openly say, that no man's uprightness and hopes shall deceive him, whosoever shall make himself known unto us under the seal of secrecy, and desire our Fraternity.

But to the false hypocrites, and to those that seek other things than wisdom, we say and witness by these presents publicly, we cannot be made known, and be betrayed unto them; and much less they shall be able to hurt as any manner of way without the will of God; but they shall certainly be partakers of all the punishment spoken of in our *Fama*; so their wicked counsels shall light upon themselves, and our treasures shall remain untouched and unstirred, until the Lion doth come, who will ask them for his use, and employ them for the confirmation and establishment of his kingdom. We ought therefore here to observe well, and make it known unto everyone, that God hath certainly and most assuredly concluded to send and grant to the world before her end, which presently thereupon shall ensue, such a truth, light, life and glory, as the first man Adam had, which he lost in Paradise, after which his successors were put and driven, with him, to misery wherefore there shall cease all servitude, falsehood, lies, and darkness, which by little and little, with the great world's revolution, was crept into all arts, works, and governments of men, and have darkened the most part of them. For from thence are proceeded an innumerable sort of all manner of false opinions and heresies, that scarce the wisest of all was able to know whose doctrine and opinion he should follow and embrace, and could not well and easily be discerned; seeing on the one part they were detained, hindered, and brought into errors through the respect of the philosophers and learned men, and on the other part through true experience. All the which, when it shall once be abolished and removed, and instead thereof a right and true rule instituted, then there will remain thanks unto them which have taken pains therein. But the work itself shall be attributed to the blessedness of our age.

As we now willingly confess, that many principal men by their writings will be a great furtherance unto this Reformation which is to come; so we desire not to have this honour ascribed to us, as if such work were only commanded and imposed upon us. But we confess, and witness openly with the Lord Jesus Christ, that it shall first happen that the stones shall arise, and offer their service, before there shall be any want of executors and accomplishers of God's counsel; yea, the Lord God hath already sent before certain messengers, which should testify his will, to wit, some new Stars, which do appear and are seen in the firmament in *Serpentano* and *Cygno*, which signify and give themselves known to everyone, that they are powerful *Signacula* of great weighty matters." So then, the secret hid writings and characters are most necessary for all such things which are found out by men. Although that great book of nature stands open to all men, yet there are but few that can read and understand the same. For as there is given to man two instruments to hear, likewise two to see, and two to smell, but only one to speak, and it were but vain to expect speech from the ears, or hearing from the eyes. So there hath been ages or times which have seen, there have also been ages that have heard, smelt, and tasted. Now there remains yet that which in short time, honour shall be likewise given to the tongue, and by the same; what before times hath been seen, heard, and smelt, now finally shall be spoken and uttered forth, when the World shall awake out of her heavy and drowsy sleep, and with an open heart, bare-head, and bare-foot, shall merrily and joyfully meet the new arising Sun.

These characters and letters, as God hath here and there incorporated them in the Holy Scriptures, the Bible, so hath he imprinted them most apparently into the wonderful creation of heaven and earth, yea in all beasts. So that like as the mathematician and astronomer can long before see and know the eclipses which are to come, so we may verily foreknow and foresee the darkness of obscurations of the church, and how long they shall last. From the which characters or letters we have borrowed our magic writing, and have found out, and made, a new language for ourselves, in the which withall is expressed and declared the nature of all things. So that it is no wonder that we are not so eloquent in other languages, the which we know that they are altogether disagreeing to the language of our forefathers, Adam and Enoch, and were through the Babylonical confusion wholly hidden.

But we must also let you understand that there are yet some Eagles' Feathers in our way, the which do hinder our purpose. Wherefore we do admonish everyone for to read diligently and continually the Holy Bible, for he that taketh all his pleasures therein, he shall know that he prepared for himself an excellent way to come to our Fraternity. For as this is the whole sum and content of our rule, that every letter or character which is in the world ought to be learned and regarded well; so those are like unto us, and are very near allied unto us, who do make the Holy Bible a rule of their life, and an aim and end of all their studies: yea to let it be a compendium and content of the whole world. And not only to have it continually in the mouth, but to know how to apply and direct the true understanding of into all times and ages of the world. Also, it is not our custom to prostitute and make so common the Holy Scriptures; for there are innumerable expounders of the same; some alleging and wresting it to serve for their opinion, some to scandal it, and most wickedly do liken it to a nose of wax, which alike should serve the divines, philosophers, physicians, and mathematicians, against all the which we do openly witness and acknowledge, that from the beginning of the world there hath not been given 'Into men a more worthy, a more excellent, and more admirable and wholesome Book than the Holy Bible. Blessed is he that hath the same, yet more blessed is he who reads it diligently, but most blessed of all is he that truly understand eth the same, for he is most like to God, and doth come most near to him. But whatsoever hath been said in the *Fama* concerning the deceivers against the transmutation of metals, and the highest medicine in the world, the same is thus to be understood, that this so great gift of God we do in no manner set at naught, or despise it. But because she bringeth not with her always the knowledge of Nature, but this bringeth forth not only medicine, but also maketh manifest and open unto us innumerable secrets and wonders. Therefore it is requisite, that we be earnest to attain to the understanding and knowledge of philosophy. And moreover, excellent wits ought not to be drawn to the tincture of metals, before they be exercised well in the knowledge of Nature. He must needs be an insatiable creature, who is come so far, that neither poverty nor sickness can hurt him, yea, who is exalted above all other men, and hath rule over that, the which doth anguish, trouble and pain others, yet will give himself again to idle things, as to build houses, make wars, and use all manner of pride, because he hath gold and silver infinite store.

God is far otherwise pleased, for he exalteth the lowly, and pulleth down the proud with disdain; to those which are of few words, he sendeth his holy Angel to speak with them, but the unclean babblers he driveth in the wilderness and solitary places. The which is the right reward of the Romish seducers, who have vomited forth their blasphemies against Christ, and as yet do not abstain from their lies in this clear shining light. In Germany all their abominations and detestable tricks have been disclosed, that thereby he may fully fulfil the measure of sin, and draw near to the end of his punishment. Therefore one day it will come to pass, that the mouth of those vipers will be stopped and the three double horn will be brought to nought, as thereof at our meeting shall more plain and at large be discoursed.

For conclusion of our Confession, we must earnestly admonish you, that you put away, if not all, yet the most books written by false Alchemists, who do think it but a jest, or a pastime, when they either misuse the Holy Trinity, when they do apply it to vain things, or deceive the people with most strange figures, and dark sentences and speeches, and cozen the simple of their money; as there are nowadays too many such books set forth, which the Enemy of man's welfare doth daily, and will to the end, mingle among the good seed, thereby to make the Truth more difficult to be believed, which in herself is simple, easy, and naked, but contrarily Falsehood is proud, haughty, and coloured with a kind of lustre of seeming godly and of humane wisdom. Ye that are wise eschew such books, and turn unto us, who seek not your moneys, but offer unto you most willingly our great treasures. We hunt not after your goods with invented lying tinctures, but desire to make you partakers of our goods. We speak unto you by parables, but would willingly bring you to the right, simple, easy and ingenuous exposition, understanding, declaration, and knowledge of all secrets. We desire not to be received of you, but invite you unto our more than kingly houses and palaces, and that verily not by our own proper motion, but (that you likewise may know it) as forced unto it, by the instigation of the Spirit of God, by his admonitions, and by the occasion of this present time.

What think you, loving people, and how seem you affected, seeing that you now understand and know, that we acknowledge ourselves truly and sincerely to profess Christ, condemn the Pope, addict ourselves to the true Philosophy, lead a Christian life, and daily call, entreat and invite many more unto our Fraternity, unto whom the same Light of God likewise appeareth? Consider you not at length how you might begin with us, not only by pondering the Gifts which are in you, and by experience which you have in the word of God, beside the careful consideration of the imperfection of all arts, and many other unfitting things, to seek for an amendment therein; to appease God, and to accommodate you for the time wherein you live. Certainly if you will perform the same, this profit will follow, that all those goods which Nature hath in all parts of the world wonderfully dispersed, shall at one time altogether be given unto you, and shall easily disburden you of all that which obscureth the understanding of man, and hindereth the working thereof, like unto the vain eccentrics and epicycles.

But those pragmatical and busy-headed men, who either are blinded with the glittering of gold, or (to say more truly) who are now honest, but by thinking such great riches should never fail, might easily be corrupted, and brought to idleness, and to riotous proud living, those we desire that they would not trouble us with their idle and vain crying. But let them think, that although there be a medicine to be had which might fully cure all diseases, nevertheless those whom God hath destined to plague with diseases, and to keep under the rod of correction, such shall never obtain any such medicine.

Even in such manner, although we might enrich the whole world, and endue them with learning, and might release it from innumerable miseries, yet shall we never be manifested and made known unto any man, without the especial pleasure of God; yea, it shall be so far from him whosoever thinks to get the benefit and be partaker of our riches and knowledge, without and against the will of God, that he shall sooner lose his life in seeking and searching for us, than to find us, and attain to come to the wished happiness of the Fraternity of the Rosy Cross.

THE CHEMICAL WEDDING OF CHRISTIAN ROSENKRUETZ

THE FIRST DAY

On an evening before Easter-day, I sat at a table, and having (as my custom was) in my humble prayer sufficiently conversed with my Creator, and considered many great mysteries (whereof the Father of Lights his Majesty had shewn me not a few) and being now ready to prepare in my heart, together with my dear Paschal Lamb, a small, unleavened, undefiled cake; All on a sudden ariseth so horrible a tempest, that I imagined no other but that through its mighty force, the hill whereon my little house was founded, would flye in pieces. But in as much as this, and the like from the Devil (who had done me many a spight) was no new thing to me, I took courage, and persisted in my meditation, till some body after an unusual manner, touched me on the back; whereupon I was so hugely terrified, that I durst hardly look about me; yet I shewed myself as cheerful as (in the like occurrence.) humane frailty would permit; now the same thing still twitching me several times. by the coat, I looked back, and behold it was a fair and glorious lady, whose garments were all skye-colour, and curiously (like Heaven) bespangled with golden stars, in her right hand she bare a trumpet of beaten gold, whereon a Name was ingraven which I could well read in but am as yet forbidden to reveal it. In her left hand she had a great bundle of letters of all languages, which she (as I afterwards understood) was to carry into all countries. She had also large and beautiful wings, full of eyes throughout, wherewith she could mount aloft, and flye swifter than any eagle. I might perhaps been able to take further notice of her, but because she stayed so small time with me, and terror and amazement still possessed me, I was fain to be content. For as soon as I turned about, she turned her letters over and over, and at length drew out a small one, with which great reverence she laid down upon the table, and without giving one word, departed from me. But in her mounting upward, she gave so mighty a blast on her gallant trumpet, that the whole hill echoed thereof, and for a full quarter of an hour after, I could hardly hear my own words.

In so unlooked for an adventure I was at a loss, how either to advise, or assist my poor self, and therefore fell upon my knees and besought my Creator to permit nothing contrary to my eternal happiness to befall me; whereupon with fear and trembling, I went to the letter, which was now so heavy, as had it been mere gold, it could hardly have been so weighty. Now as I we. diligently viewing it, I found a little seal, whereupon a curious cross with this inscription, IN HOC SIGNO VINCES (In this sign you will be victorious.) was ingraven. Now as soon as I espied this sign I was the more comforted, as not being ignorant that such a seal was little acceptable, and much less useful, to the Devil. Whereupon I tenderly opened the letter, and within it, in an azure field, in golden letters, found the following verses written.

"This day, this day, this, this
The Royal Wedding is.
Art thou thereto by birth inclin'd,

And unto joy of God design'd,
Then may'st thou to the mountain trend,
Whereon three stately temples stand,
And there see all from end to end.
Keep watch, and ward,
Thy self regard;
Unless with diligence thou bathe,
The Wedding can't thee harmless save;
He'l damage have that here delays;
Let him beware, too light that weighs."
Underneath stood Sponsus and Sponsa. (Bridegroom and Bride)

As soon as I had read this letter, I was presently like to have fainted away, all my hair stood on end, and a cold sweat trickled down my whole body. For although I well perceived that this was the appointed wedding, whereof seven years before I was acquainted in a bodily vision, and which now so long time I had with great earnestness attended (awaited), and which lastly, by the account and calculation of the planets, I had most diligently observed, I found so to be, yet could I never fore-see that it must happen under so grievous perilous conditions. For whereas I before imagined that to be a well-come and acceptable guest, I needed only be ready to appear at the wedding, I was now directed to Divine Providence, of which until this time I was never certain. I also found by my self, the more I examined my self, that in my head there was nothing but gross mis-understanding, and blindness in mysterious things, so that I was not able to comprehend even those things which lay under my feet, and which I daily conversed with, much less that I should be born to the searching out, and understanding of the secrets of Nature, since in my opinion Nature might every where find a more virtuous disciple, to whom to intrust her precious, though temporary, and changeable treasures. I found also that my bodily behaviour, and outward good conversation, and brotherly love toward my neighbour, was not duly purged and cleansed; moreover the tickling of the flesh manifested itself, whose affection was bent only to pomp and bravery, and worldly pride, and not to the good of mankind: and I was always contriving how by this art I might in a short time abundantly increase my profit and advantage, rear up stately palaces, make my self an everlasting name in the world, and other like carnal designs. But the obscure words concerning the three temples did particularly afflict me, which I was not able to make out by any after-speculation, and perhaps should not yet, had they not been wonderfully revealed to me. Thus sticking betwixt hope and fear, examining my self again and again, and finding only my own frailty and impotency, not being in any wise able to succour myself, and exceedingly amazed at the fore-mentioned threatening, at length I betook myself to my usual and most secure course; after I had finished my earnest and most fervent prayer, I laid me down in my bed, that so perchance my good angel by the Divine permission might appear, and (as it had sometimes formerly happened) instruct me in this doubtful affair, which to the praise of God, my own good, and my neighbours faithful and hearty warning and amendment did now likewise fall out. For I was yet scarce fallen asleep, when me-thought, I, together with a numberless multitude of men lay fettered with great chains in a dark dungeon, wherein without the least glimpse of light, we swarmed like bees one over another, and thus rendered each others affliction more grievous. But although neither I, nor any of the rest could see one jot, yet I continually heard one heaving himself above the other, when his chains or fetters were become ever so little lighter, though none of us had much reason to shove up the other, since we were all captive wretches. Now as I with the rest had continued a good while in this affliction, and each was still reproaching the other with his blindness and captivity, at length we heard many trumpets sounding together, and kettle drums beating so artificially thereto, that it even revived and rejoiced us in our calamity. During this noise the cover of the dungeon was from above lifted up, and a little light let down unto us. Then first might truly have been discerned the bustle we kept, for all went pesle-mesle, and he who perchance had too much heaved up himself, was forced down again under the others feet. In brief, each one strove to be uppermost, neither did I my self linger, but with my weighty fetters slipt up from under the rest, and then heaved myself upon a stone, which I laid hold of; howbeit, I was several times caught at by others, from whom yet as well as I might, with hands and feet I still guarded my self. For we imagined no other but that we should all be set at liberty, which yet fell out quite otherwise. For after the nobles who looked upon us from above through the hole, had a while recreated themselves with this our struggling and lamenting, a certain hoary-headed ancient man called us to be quiet, and having scarce obtained it, began (as I still remember) thus to say on.

"If wretched mankind would forbear
Themselves so to uphold,
Then sure on them much good confer,
My righteous Mother would:
But since the same will not ensue,
They must in care and sorrow rue,
And still in prison lie.
Howbeit, my dear Mother will
Their follies over-see,
Her choicest goods permitting still
Too much in the' light to be.
Though very rarely it may seem
That they may still keep some esteem,
Which else would pass for forgery.
Wherefore in honour of the feast
We this day solemnise,
That so her grace may be increast,
A good deed she'l devise.
For now a cord shall be let down,
And whosoe'er can hang thereon,
Shall freely be releast.

He had scarce done speaking when an ancient matron commanded her servants to let down the cord seven times into the dungeon, and draw up whosoever could hang upon it. Good God! that I could sufficiently describe the hurry and disquiet that then arose amongst us for every one strove to get to the cord, and yet only hindered each other. But after seven minutes a sign was given by a little bell, whereupon at the first pull the servants drew up four. At that time I could not come near the cord by much, having (as is before-mentioned) to my huge misfortune, betaken my self to a stone at the wall of the dungeon, and thereby was disabled to get to the cord which descended in the middle. The cord was let down the second time, but divers, because their chains were too heavy, and their hands too tender, could not keep their hold on the cord, but with themselves beat down many another, who else perhaps might have held fast enough; nay, many an one was forcibly pulled off by another, who yet could not himself get at it, so mutually envious were we even in this our great misery. But they of all others most moved my compassion, whose weight was so heavy, that they tore their very hands from their bodies, and yet could not get up. Thus it came to pass that at those five times very few were drawn up. For as soon as the sign was given, the servants were so nimble at the draught, that the most part tumbled one upon another, and the cord, this time especially, was drawn up very empty. Whereupon the greatest part, and even I myself, despaired of redemption, and called upon God that he would have pity on us, and (if possible) deliver us out of this obscurity, who also then heard some of us: for when the cord came down the sixth time, some of them hung themselves fast upon it; and whilst in the drawing up, the cord swung from one side to the other, it (perhaps by the will of God) came to me, which I suddenly catching, uppermost above all the rest, and so at length beyond hope came out; whereat I exceedingly rejoiced, so that I perceived not the wound, which in the drawing up I received on my head by a sharp stone, till I with the rest who were released (as was always before done) was fain to help at the seventh and last pull, at which time through straining, the blood ran down all over my clothes, which I

nevertheless for joy regarded not. Now when the last draught whereon the most of all hung, was finished, the matron caused the cord to be laid away, and willed her aged son to declare her resolution to the rest of the prisoners, who after he had a little bethought himself spoke, thus unto them.

"Ye children dear
All present here,
What is but now complete and done,
Was long before resolved on:
What er'r my mother of great grace
To each on both sides here hath shown,
May never discontent mix-place;
The joyful time is drawing on,
When every one shall equal be,
None wealthy, none in penury.

Who er'e receiveth great commands
Hath work enough to fill his hands.
Who er'e with much hath trusted been,
'Tis well if he may save his skin.
Wherefore your lamentations cease,
What is't to wait for some few days?"

As soon as he had finished these words, the cover was again put to and locked down, and the trumpets and kettle-drums began afresh, yet could not the noise thereof be so loud, but that the bitter lamentation of the prisoners which arose in the dungeon was heard above all, which soon also caused my eyes to run-over. Presently after the ancient matron, together with her son sat down on seats before prepared, and commanded the redeemed should be told. Now as soon as she understood the number, and had written it down in a gold-yellow tablet, she demanded every ones name, which were also written down by a little page; having viewed us all, one after another, she sighed, and spoke to her son, so as I could well hear her, "Ah how hartily am I grieved for the poor men in the dungeon! I would to God I durst release them all," whereunto her son replied; "It is mother thus ordained of God, against whom we may not contend. In case we all of us were lords, and possessed all the goods upon Earth, and were seated at table, who would there then be to bring up the service?" whereupon his mother held her peace, but soon after she said; "Well, however, let these be freed from their fetters", which was likewise presently done, and I, except a few was the last; yet I could not refrain, but (though I still looked upon the rest) bowed myself before the ancient matron, and thanked God that through her, had graciously and fatherly vouch-safed to bring me out of such darkness into the light: after me the rest did likewise, to the satisfaction of the matron. Lastly, to every one was given a piece of gold for a remembrance, and to spend by the Way, on the one whereof was stamped the rising sun, on the other (as I remember) these three letters, D.L.S.(*Deus Lux Solis (*God is the light of the sun), *Deo Laus Semper.* (God be praised for ever.)) and therewith every one had license to depart, and was sent to his own business with this annexed intimation, that we to the glory of God should benefit our neighbours, and reserve in silence what we had been intrusted with, which we also promised to do, and so departed one from another. But in regard of the wounds which the fetters had caused me, I could not well go forward, but halted on both feet, which the matron presently espying, laughing at it and calling me again to her said thus to me, "My son, let not this defect afflict thee, but call to mind thy infirmities, and therewith thank God who hath permitted thee even in this world, and in the state of thy imperfection to come into so high a light, and keep these wounds for my sake." Whereupon the trumpets began again to sound, which so affrighted me that I awoke, and then first perceived that it was only a dream, which was so strongly impressed upon my imagination, that I was still perpetually troubled about it, and me thought I was yet sensible of the wounds on my feet. Howbeit, by all these things I well understood that God had vouchsafed that I should be present at this mysterious and bidden wedding; wherefore with childlike confidence I returned thanks to his Divine Majesty, and besought him, that he would further preserve me in his fear, that he would daily fill my heart with wisdom and understanding, and at length graciously (without my desert) conduct me to the desired end. Hereupon I prepared my self for the way, put on my white linen coat, girded my loins, with a blood-red ribbon bound-cross-ways over my shoulder. In my hat I stuck four red roses, that I might the sooner by this token be taken notice of Amongst the throng. For food I took bread, salt and water, which by the counsel of an understanding person I had at certain times used, not without profit, in the like occurrences. But before I parted from my cottage, I first in this my dress and wedding garment, fell down upon my knees, and besought God, that in case such a thing were, he would vouchsafe me a good issue. And thereupon in the presence of God I made a Vow, that if any thing through his grace should be revealed unto me, I would employ it neither to my own honour nor authority in the world, but to the spreading of his Name, and the service of my neighbour. And with this vow, and good hope I departed out of my cell with joy.

THE SECOND DAY

I was hardly got out of my cell into a forest when me thought the whole heaven and all the elements had already trimmed themselves against (in preparation for) this wedding. For even the birds chanted more pleasantly then before, and the young fawns skipped so merrily, that they rejoiced my old heart, and moved me to sing: wherefore with a loud voice I thus began:

"With mirth thou pretty bird rejoice,
Thy Maker's praise in-tranced.
Lift up thy shrill and pleasant voice,
Thy God is high advanced.
Thy food before he did provide,
And gives it in a fitting side,
Therewith be thou sufficed.
Why should'st thou now unpleasant be,
Thy wrath against God venting?
That he a little bird made thee,
Thy silly head tormenting?
Because he made thee not a man,
O peace, he hath well thought thereon.
Therewith be thou sufficed.
What is't I'd have poor earthly worm,
By God (as'twere) inditing,
That I should thus 'gainst Heaven storm
To force great arts by fighting?
God will out-braved be by none,
Who's good for naught, may hence be gone,
O man b' herewith sufficed.
That he no Caesar hath thee fram'd,
To pine therefore 'tis needless
His name perhaps thou hadst defam'd
Whereof he was not heedless
Most clear and bright Gods eyes do shine,
He pierces to thy heart within,
And cannot be deceived."

This sang I now from the bottom of my heart throughout the whole forest, so that it resounded from all parts, and the hills repeated my last words, until at length I espied a curious green heath, wither I betook my self out of the forest. Upon this heath stood three lovely tall cedars, which by reason of their breadth afforded an excellent and desired shade, whereat I greatly rejoiced; for although I had not hitherto gone far, yet my earnest longing made me very faint, whereupon I hasted to the trees to rest a little under them, but as soon as I came somewhat higher, I espied a tablet fastened to one of them, on which (as afterwards I read) in curious letters the following words were written:

"God save thee, stranger! If thou hast heard anything concerning the nuptials of the King, consider these words. By us doth the Bridegroom offer thee a choice between four ways, all of which, if thou dost not sink down in the way, can bring thee to his royal court. The first is short but dangerous, and one which will lead thee into rocky places, through which it will be scarcely possible to pass. The second is longer, and takes thee circuitously; it is plain and easy, if by the help of the Magnet, thou turnest neither to left nor right. The third is that truly royal way which through various pleasures and pageants of our King, affords thee a joyful journey; but this so far has scarcely been allotted to one in a thousand. By the fourth shall no man reach the place, because it is a consuming way, practicable only for incorruptible bodies. Choose now which thou wilt of the three, and persevere constantly therein, for know which soever thou shalt enter, that is the one destined for thee by immutable Fate, nor canst thou go back therein save at great peril to life. These are the things which we would have thee know, but, ho, beware! thou knowest not with how much danger thou cost commit thyself to this way, for if thou knowest thyself by the smallest fault to be obnoxious to the laws of our King, I beseech thee, while it is still possible, to return swiftly to thy house by the way thou camest."

As soon as I had read this writing all my joy was near vanished again, and I who before sang merrily, began now inwardly to lament. For although I saw all the three ways before me, and understood that hence forward it was vouchsafed me, to make choice of one of them, yet it troubled me that in case I went the stony and rocky way, I might get a miserable and deadly fall, or taking the long one, I might wander out of it through by-ways, or be otherway's detained in the great journey. Neither durst I hope, that I amongst thousands should be the very one who should choose the royal way. I saw likewise the fourth before me, but it was so invironed with fire and exhalations, that I durst not (by much) draw near it, and therefore again and again considered, whether I should turn back, or take any of the ways before me. I well weighted my own unworthiness, but the dream still comforted me, that I was delivered out of the tower, and yet I durst not confidently rely upon a dream; whereupon I was so variously perplexed, that for very great weariness, hunger and thirst seized me, whereupon I presently drew out my bread, cut a slice of it, which a snow-white dove of whom I was not aware, sitting upon the tree, espied and therewith (perhaps according to her wonted manner) came down, and betook herself very familiarly with me, to whom I willingly imparted my food, which she received, and so with her prettiness did again a little refresh me. But as soon as her enemy a most black raven perceived it, he straight darted himself down upon the dove, and taking no notice of me, would needs force away the dove's meat, who could no otherwise guard her self but by flight; whereupon they both together flew towards the south, at which I was so hugely incensed and grieved, that without thinking what I did, I made hast after the filthy raven, and so against my will ran into one of the forementioned ways a whole fields length; and thus the raven being chased away, and the dove delivered, I then first observed what I had inconsiderately done, and that I was already entered into a way, from which under peril of great punishment I durst not retire. And though I had still herewith in some measure to comfort my self, yet that which was worst of all to me, was, that I had left my bag and bread at the tree, and could never retrieve them. For as soon as I turned my self about, a contrary wind was so strong against me, that it was ready to fell me. But if I went forward on my way, I perceived no hinderance at all. From whence I could easily conclude, that it would cost me my life, in case I should set my self against the wind, wherefore I patiently took up my cross, got up on my feet, and resolved, since so it must be, I would use my utmost endeavour to get to my journeys end before night. Now although many apparent byways shewed themselves, yet I still proceeded with my compass, and would not budge one step from the Meridian Line; howbeit the way was oftentimes so rugged and unpassable, that I was in no little doubt of it. On this way I constantly thought upon the dove and raven, and yet could not search out the meaning until at length upon a high hill afar off I espied a stately portal, to which not regarding how far it was distant both from me and the way I was in, I hasted, because the sun had already hid himself under the hills, and I could elsewhere espy no abiding place, and this verily I ascribe only to God, who might well have permitted me to go forward in this way, and withheld my eyes that so I might have gazed beside this gate. To which I now made mighty haste, and reached it by so much daylight, as to take a very competent view of it. Now it was an exceeding royal beautiful portal, whereon were carved a multitude of most noble figures and devices, every one of which (as I afterwards learned) had its peculiar signification. Above was fixed a pretty large tablet, with these words, *Procul hinc, procul ite profani*, (Begone, begone, ye who are not called.) and other things more, that I was earnestly forbidden to relate. Now as soon as I was come under the portal, there straight stepped forth one in a sky-coloured habit, whom I in friendly manner saluted, which though he thankfully returned, yet he instantly demanded of me my letter of invitation. O how glad was I that I had then brought it with me. For how easily might I have forgotten it (as it also chanced to others) as he himself told me' I quickly presented it, wherewith he was not only satisfied, but (at which I much wondered) shewed me abundance of respect, saying, Come in my brother, an acceptable guest you are to me; and withal intreated me not to with-hold my name from him. Now having replied, that I was a Brother of the Red-Rosie Cross, he both wondered, and seemed to rejoice at it, and then proceeded thus, My brother, have you nothing about you wherewith to purchase a token? I answered my ability was small, but if he saw any thing about me he had a mind to, it was at his service. Now he having requested of me my bottle of water, and I granted it he gives me a golden token whereon stood no more but these two letters, S. C., (*Santitate Constantia*, Steadfastness in piety; *Sponsus Charus*, Well beloved bridegroom; *Spes Charia*, hope and love.) intreating me that when it stood me in good stead, I would remember him. After which I asked him, how many were got in before me, which he also told me, and lastly out of mere friendship gave me a sealed letter to the second Porter. Now having lingered some time with him, the night grew on. Whereupon a great beacon upon the gates was immediately fired, that so if any were still upon the way, he might make hasted hither. But the way where it finished at the castle, was on both sides inclosed with walls, and planted with all sorts of excellent fruit trees, and still on every third tree on each side lanterns were hung up, wherein all the candles were already lighted with a glorious torch by a beautiful Virgin, habited in skye-colour, which was so noble and majestic a spectacle, that I yet delayed somewhat longer than was requisite. But at length after sufficient information, and an advantageous instruction, I friendly departed from the first Porter. On the way, though I would gladly have known what was written in my letter, yet since I had no reason to mistrust the Porter, I forbare my purpose, and so went on the way, until I came likewise to the second gate, which though it was very like the other, yet was it adorned with images and mystic significations. In the affixed tablet stood *Date et dabitur vobis.* (Give and it will be given to you) Under this gate lay a terrible grim lion chain'd, who as soon as he espied me arose and made at me with great roaring; whereupon the second Porter who lay upon a stone of marble awaked, and wished me not to be troubled or affrighted, and then drove back the lion, and having received the letter which I with trembling reached him, he read it, and with very great respect spake thus to me, "Now well-come in Gods Name unto me the man whom of long time I would gladly have seen." Meanwhile he also drew out a token, and asked me whether I could purchase it? But having nothing else left but my salt, presented it to him, which he thankfully accepted. Upon this token again stood only two letters, namely, S. M.(*Studio Merentis*, To the worthy in study; *Sal Humor Sponso Mittendus,* pawn of the bridegroom; *Sal Mineralis,* mineral salt; *Sal Menstrualis,* salt of purification) Being now just about to enter discourse with him, it began to ring in the castle, whereupon the Porter counselled me to run apace, or else all the pains and labour I had hitherto taken would serve to no purpose, for the lights above began already to be extinguished; whereupon I dispatched with such haste that I heeded not the Porter, in such anguish was I, and truly it was but necessary, for I could not run so fast but that the Virgin, after whom all the lights were put out, was at my heels, and I should never have found the way, had not she with her torch afforded me some light; I was moreover constrained to enter the very next to her, and the gate was so suddenly clap's to, that a part of my coat was locked out, which I was verily forced to leave behind me; for neither I, nor they who stood ready without and called at the gate could prevail with the Porter to open it again, but he delivered the keys to the Virgin, who took them with her into the court. Mean time I again surveyed the gate, which now appeared so rich, as the whole world could not equal it; just by the door were two columns on one of which stood a pleasant figure with this inscription,

Congratulor. The other having its countenance veiled was sad, and beneath was written, Condoleo. In brief, the inscriptions and figures thereon, were so dark and mysterious, that the most dexterous man upon earth could not have expounded them. But all these (if God permit) I shall ever long publish and explain. Under this gate I was again to give my name, which was this last time written down in a little vellum book, and immediately with the rest dispatched to the Lord Bridegroom. Here it was where I first received the true guest token, which was somewhat less than the former, but yet much heavier.

Upon this stood these letters, S. P. N. Besides this, a new pair of shoes were given me, for the floor of the castle was laid with pure shining marble; my old shoes I was to give away to one of the poor who sate in throngs, howbeit in very good order, under the gate. I then bestowed them on an old man; after which two pages with as many torches conducted me into a little room; there they willed me to sit down on a form, which I did, but they sticking their torches in two holes, made in the pavement, departed and thus left me sitting alone. Soon after I heard a noise, but saw nothing, and it proved to be certain men who stumbled in upon me; but since I could see nothing, I was fain to suffer, and attend what they would do with me; but presently perceiving them to be barbers, I intreated them not to jostle me so, for I was content to do whatever they desired, whereupon they quickly let me go, and so one of them (whom I could not yet see) fine and gently cut away the hair-round about from the crown of my head, but on my forehead, ears and eyes he permitted my ice-grey locks to hang. In his first encounter (I must confess) I was ready to dispair, for inasmuch as some of them shoved me so forceably, and I could yet see nothing, I could think no other but that God for my curiosity had suffered me to miscarry. Now these invisible barbers carefully gathered up the hair which was cut off, and carried it away with them. After which the two pages entered again, and heartily laughed at me for being so terrified. But they had scarce spoken a few words with me, when again a little bell began to ring, which (as the pages informed me) was to give notice for assembling; whereupon they willed me to rise, and through many walks, doors and winding stairs lighted me into a spacious hall. In this room was a great multitude of guests, emperors, kings, princes, and lords, noble and ignoble, rich and poor, and all sorts of people, at which I hugely marvelled, and thought to my self, ah, how gross a fool hast thou been to engage upon this journey with so much bitterness and toil, when (behold) here are even those fellows whom thou well know'st, and yet hadst never any reason to esteem. They are now all here, and thou with all thy prayers and supplications art hardly got in at last. This and more the Devil at that time injected, whom I notwithstanding (as well as I could) directed to the issue. Mean time one or other of my acquaintance here and there spoke to me: Oh Brother Rosencreutz! Art thou here too; yea, (my brethren) replied I, the grace of God hath helped me in also; at which they raised a mighty laughter, looking upon it as ridiculous that there should be need of God in so slight an occasion. Now having demanded each of them concerning his way, and found that most were forced to clamber over the rocks, certain trumpets (none of which we yet saw) began to sound to the table, whereupon they all seated themselves, every one as he judged himself above the rest; so that for me and some other sorry fellows there was hardly a little nook left at the lower-most table. Presently the two pages entered, and one of them said grace in so handsom and excellent manner, as rejoyced the very heart in my body.

Howbeit, certain great St John's made but little reckoning of them, but fleired and winked one at another, biting their lips within their hats, and using more the like unseemly gestures. After this, meat was brought in, and albeit none could be seen, yet every thing was so orderly managed, that it seemed to me as if every guest had had his proper attendant. Now my artists having somewhat recruited themselves, and the wine having a little removed shame from their hearts, they presently began to vaunt and brag of their abilities. One would prove this, another that, and commonly the most sorry idiots made the loudest noise. Ah, when I call to mind what preternatural and impossible enterprises I then heard, I am still ready to vomit at it. In fine, they never kept in their order, but when ever one rascal here, another there, could insinuate himself in between the nobles; then pretended they the finishing of such adventures as neither Sampson, nor yet Hercules with all their strength could ever have achieved: this would discharge Atlas of his burden; the other would again draw forth the three-headed Cerberus out of Hell. In brief, every man had his own prate, and yet the great lords were so simple that they believed their pretences, and the rogues so audacious, that although one or other of them was here and there rapped over the fingers with a knife, yet they flinched not at it, but when any one perchance had filched a gold-chain, then would all hazard for the like. I saw one who heard the rustling of the heavens. The second could see Plato's ideas. A third could number Democritus's atoms. There were also not a few pretenders to the perpetual motion. Many an one (in my opinion) had good understanding, but assumed too much to himself, to his own destruction Lastly, there was one also who would needs out of hand persuade us that he saw the servitors who attended, and would still have pursued his contention, had not one of those invisible waiters reached him so handsom a cuff upon his lying muzzle, that not only he, but many more who were by him, became as mute as mice. But it best of all pleased me, that all those, of whom I had any esteem, were very quiet in their business, and made no loud cry of it, but acknowledged themselves to be misunderstanding men, to whom the mysteries of nature were too high, and they themselves much too small. In this tumult I had almost cursed the day wherein I came hither; for I could not but with anguish behold that those lewd vain people were above at the board, but I in so sorry a place could not rest in quiet, one of those rascals scornfully reproaching me for a motley fool. Now I thought not that there was yet one gate behind, through which we must pass, but imagined I was during the whole wedding, to continue in this scorn, contempt and indignity, which yet I had at no time deserved, either of the Lord Bridegroom or the Bride. And therefore (in my opinion) he should have done well to sort out some other fool to his wedding than me. Behold, to such impatience cloth the iniquity of this world reduce simple hearts. But this really was one part of my lameness, whereof (as is before mentioned) I dreamed. And truly this clamour the longer it lasted, the more it increased. For there were already those who boasted of false and imaginary visions, and would persuade us of palpably lying dreams. Now there sat by me a very fine quiet man, who oftentimes discoursed of excellent matters. At length he said, "Behold my brother, if any one should now come who were willing to instruct these blockish people in the right way, would he be heard? "No, verily," replied I. "The world" said he, "is now resolved (whatever comes on it) to be cheated, and cannot abide to give ear to those who intend its good. Seest thou also that same cocks-comb, with what whimsical figures and foolish conceits he allures others to him. There one makes mouths at the people with the unheard-of mysterious words. Yet believe me in this, the time is now coming when those shameful vizards shall be plucked off, and all the world shall know what vagabond imposters were concealed behind them. Then perhaps that will be valued which at present is not esteemed. "Whilst he was thus speaking, and the clamour the longer it lasted the worse it was, all on a sudden there began in the hall such excellent and stately musick, as all the days of my life I never heard the like; whereupon every one held his peace, and attended what would become of it. Now there were in this music all sorts of stringed instruments imaginable, which sounded together in such harmony, that I forgot myself, and sat so unmovable, that those who sat by me were amazed at me, and this lasted near half an hour, wherein none of us spoke one word. For as soon as ever any one was about to open his mouth, he got an unexpected blow, neither knew he from whence it came. Me thought since we were not permitted to see the musicians, I should have been glad to view only all the instruments they made use of. After half an hour this music ceased unexpectedly, and we could neither see nor hear any thing further. Presently after, before the door of the hall began a great noise sounding and beating of trumpets, shalms and kettle-drums, also master-like, as if the Emperor of Rome had been entering; whereupon the door opened of itself, and then the noise of the trumpets was so loud, that we were hardly able to indure it. Meanwhile (to my thinking) many thousand small tapers came into the hall, all which of themselves marched in so very exact an order as altogether amazed us, till at last the two aforementioned pages with bright torches, lighting in a most beautiful Virgin, all drawn on a gloriously gilded triumphant self-moving throne, entered the hall. It seemed to me she was the very same who before on the way kindled, and put out the lights, and that these her attendants were the very same whom she formerly placed at the trees. She was not now as before in skye-colour, but arrayed in a snow-white glittering robe, which sparkled of pure gold, and cast such a lustre that we durst not steadily behold it. Both the pages were after the same manner habited (albeit somewhat more slightly). As soon as they were come into the middle of the hall, and were descended from the throne, all the small tapers made obeisance before her. Whereupon we all stood up from our benches, yet every one staid in his own place. Now she having to us, and we again to her, shewed all respect and reverence, in a most pleasant tone she began thus to speak;

"The King my Lord most gracious,
Who now's not very far from us,
As also his most lovely Bride,
To him in troth and honour ti'd;
Already, with great joy indu'd,
Have your arrival hither view'd;
And do to every one,
and all Promise their grace in special;
And from their very hearts desire,
You may it at the same acquire;
That so their future nuptial joy
May mixed be with none's annoy."
Hereupon with all her small tapers she again courteously bowed, and presently after began thus:
"In the invitation writ, you know
That no man called was hereto
Who of God's rarest gifts good store
Had not received long before,
Adorned with all requisit's,
As in such cases it befit's.
How though they cannot well conceit
That any man's so desperate,
Under conditions so hard,
Here to intrude without regard;
Unless he have been first of all,
Prepared for this nuptial;
And therefore in good hopes do dwell
That with all you it will be well.
Yet men are grown so bold, and rude,
Not weighing their inepitude,
As still to thrust themselves in place
Whereto none of them called was.
No cocks-comb here himself may sell,
No rascal in with others steal;
For they resolve without all let
A wedding pure to celebrate.
So then the artists for to weigh
Seals shall be fix'd the ensuing day;

Whereby each one may lightly find
What he hath left at home behind.
If here be any of that rout
Who have good cause themselves to doubt,
Let him seek quickly hence aside;
For that in ease he longer bide,
Of grace forelor'n, and quite undone
Betimes he must the gauntlet run.
If any now his conscience gall,
He shall tonight be left in th' hall
And be again releas't by morn,
Yet so he hither ne'er return.
If any man have confidence,
He with his waiter may go hence,
Who shall him to his chamber light
Where he may rest in peace tonight;
And there with praise await the scale
Or else his sleep may chance to fail.
The others here may take it well,
For who aim's 'bove what's possible,
'Twere better much he hence had pas't,
But of you all wee'l hope the best."

As soon as she had done speaking this, she again made reverence, and sprung cheerfully into her throne, after which the trumpets began again to sound, which yet was not of force to take from many their grievous sighs. So they again conducted her invisibly away, but the most part of the small tapers remained in the room, and still one of them accompanied each of us. In such perturbation 'tis not well possible to express what pensive thoughts and gestures were amongst us. Yet the most part were resolved to await the scale, and in ease things sorted not well, to depart (as they hoped) in peace. I had soon cast up my reckoning, and being my conscience convinced me of all ignorance, and unworthiness, I purposed to stay with the rest in the hall, and chose much rather to content myself with the meal I had already taken, than to run the risk of a future repulse. Now after that every one by his small taper had severally been conducted into a chamber (each as I since understood into a peculiar one), there stayed nine of us, and amongst the rest he also, who discoursed with me at the table. But although our small tapers left us not, yet soon after within an hours time one of the aforementioned pages came in, and bringing a great bundle of cords with him, first demanded of us whether we had concluded to stay there, which when we had with sighs affirmed, he bound each of us in a several place, and so went away with our small tapers, and left us poor wretches in darkness. Then some first began to perceive the imminent danger, and I my self could not refrain tears. For although we were not forbidden to speak, yet anguish and affliction suffered none of us to utter one word. For the cords were so wonderfully made, yet none could cut them, much less get them off his feet. Yet this comforted me, that still the future gain, of many an one, who had now betaken himself to rest, would prove very little to his satisfaction. But we by only one nights penance might expiate all our presumption; till at length in my sorrowful thoughts I fell asleep, during which I had a dream. Now although there be no great matter in it, yet I esteem it not impertinent to recount it. Me thought I was upon an high mountain, and saw before me a great and large valley. In this valley were gathered together an unspeakable multitude of people, each of which had at his head a thread, by which he was hanged up towards Heaven, now one hung high, another low, some stood even quite upon the earth. But in the air there flew up and down an ancient man, who had in his hand a pair of sheers, wherewith here he cut one's, and there another's thread. Now he that was nigh the earth was so much the readier, and fell without noise, but when it happened to one of the high ones, he fell, so that the earth quaked. To some it came to pass that their thread was no stretched, that they came to the earth before the thread was cut. I took pleasure in this tumbling, and it joyed me at the heart, when he who had over-exalted himself in the air, of his wedding, got so shameful a fall, that it carried even some of his neighbours along with him. In like manner it also rejoiced me, that he who had all this while kept himself near the earth, could come down so fine and gently, that even his next men perceived it not. But being now in my highest fit of jolity, I was unawares jogged by one of my fellow captives, upon which I was awaked, and was very much discontented with him. Howbeit, I considered my dream, and recounted it to my brother, who lay by me on the other side, who was not dissatisfied with it, but hoped some comfort might thereby be pretended. In such discourse we spent the remaining part of the night, and with longing expected the day.

THE THIRD DAY

Now as soon as the lovely day was broken, and the bright sun, having raised himself above the hills, had again betaken himself, in the high heaven, to his appointed office, my good champions began to rise out of their beds, and leisurely to make themselves ready unto the inquisition. Whereupon, one after another, they came again into the hall, and giving us a good morrow, demanded how we had slept; and having espied our bonds, there were some that reproved us for being so cowardly, and that we had not, as they, hazarded upon all adventures. Howbeit, same of them whose hearts still smote them made no loud cry of the business. We excused ourselves with our ignorance, hoping we should now be set at liberty, and learn wit by this disgrace, that they on the contrary had not yet altogether escaped, and perhaps their greatest danger was still to be expected. At length each one being assembled, the trumpets began now again to sound and the kettle drums to beat as formerly, and we then imagined no other but that the Bridegroom was ready to present himself; which nevertheless was a huge mistake. For it was again the yesterday's Virgin who had arrayed her self all in red velvet, and girded her self with a white scarfe. Upon her head she had a green wreath of laurel, which hugely became her. Her train was now no more of small tapers, but consisted of two hundred men in harness, who were all (like her) cloathed in red and white. Now as soon as they were alighted from the throne, she comes straight to us prisoners, and after she had saluted us, she said in few words, "That some of you have been sensible of your wretched condition is hugely pleasing to my most mighty Lord, and he is also resolved you shall fare the better for it." And having espied me in my habit, she laughed and spake, "Good lack! Hast thou also submitted thy self to the yoke, I imagined thou wouldst have made thy self very smug," with which words she caused my eyes to run over. After which she commanded we should be unbound, and coupled together and placed in a station where we might well behold the scales. "For," said she, "it may yet fare better with them, than the presumptuous, who yet stand here at liberty." Mean time the scales which were intirely of gold were hung up in the midst of the hall. There was also a little table covered with red velvet, and seven weights placed thereon. First of all stood a pretty great one, next four little ones; lastly, two great ones severally. And these weights in proportion to their bulk were so heavy, that no man can believe or comprehend it. But each of the harnessed men had together with a naked sword a strong rope. These she distributed according to the number; of weights into seven bands and out of every band chose one for their proper weight; and then again sprung up into her high throne. Now as soon as she had made her reverence, with a very shrill tone she began thus to speak:

"Who int' a painters room does go
And nothing does of painting know,
Yet does in prating thereof, pride it;
Shall be of all the world derided.
Who into th' artists order goes,
And "hereunto was never chose;
Yet with pretence of skill does pride it;
Shall be of all the world derided.
Who at a wedding does appear,
And yet was ner'e intended there;
Yet does in coming highly pride it;
Shall be of all the world derided.
Who now into this scale ascends,
The weights not proving his fast friends,
And that it bounces so does ride it;
Shall be of all the world derided."

As soon as the Virgin had done speaking, one of the Pages commanded each one to place himself according to his order, and one after another to step in: which one of the emperors made no scruple of, but first of all bowed himself a little towards the Virgin, and afterwards in all his stately attire went up: whereupon each captain laid in his weight; which (to the wonder of all) he stood out. But the last was too heavy for him, so that forth he must, and that with much anguish that (as it seemed to me) the Virgin her self had pity on him, who also beckoned to her people to hold their peace, yet was the good emperor bound and delivered over to the sixth band. Next him again came forth another emperor, who steps hautily into the scale, and having a great thick book under his gown, he imagined not to fail. But being scarce able to abide the third weight, and being unmercifully flung down, and his book in that affrightment flipping from him, all the soldiers began to laugh, and he was delivered up bound to the third band. Thus it went also with some others of the emperors who were all shamefully laughed at and captived. After these comes forth a little short man with a curled brown beard, an emperor too, who after the usual reverence got up also, and held out so steadfastly, that me thought, and there been more weights ready, he would have outstood them; to whom the Virgin immediately arose, and bowed before him, causing him to put on a gown of red velvet, and at last reached him a branch of laurel, having good store of them upon her throne, upon the steps whereof she willed him to sit down. Now how, after him it fared with the rest of the emperors, kings and lords, would be too long to recount; but I cannot leave unmentioned that few of those great personages held out. Howbeit sundry eminent virtues (beyond my hopes) were found in many. One could stand out this, the second another, some two, some three, four or five, but few could attain to the just perfection; but everyone who failed, was miserably laughed at by the bands. After the inquisition had also passed over the gentry, the learned, and unlearned, and the rest, and in each condition perhaps one, it may be, two, but for the most part none, was found perfect, it came at length to those honest gentlemen the vagabond cheaters, and rascally *Lapidem Spitalanficum* makers, who were set upon the scale with such scorn, that I my self for all my grief was ready to burst my belly with laughing, neither could the very prisoners themselves refrain. For the most part could not abide that severe trial, but with whips and scourges were jerked out of the scale, and led to the other prisoners, yet to a suitable band. Thus of so great a throng so few remained, that I am ashamed to discover their number. Howbeit there were persons of quality also amongst them, who notwithstanding were (like the rest) honoured with velvet robes and wreaths of laurel.

The inquisition being completely finished, and none but we poor coupled hounds standing aside, at length one of the captains stepped forth, and said, Gratious Madam, if it please your ladyship let these poor men, who acknowledged their mis-understanding, be set upon the scale also without their incurring any danger of penalty, and only for recreation's sake, if perchance any thing that is right may be found amongst them. In the first place I was in great perplexity, for in my anguish this was my only comfort, that I was not to stand in such ignominy, or to be lashed out of the scale. For I nothing doubted but that many of the prisoners wished that they had stay'd ten nights with us in the hall. Yet since the Virgin consented, so it must be, and we being untied were one after another set up. Now although the most part miscarried, yet they were neither laughed at, nor scourged, but peaceably placed on one side. My companion was the fifth, who held out bravely, whereupon all, but especially the captain who made the request for us, applauded him, and the Virgin shewed him the usual respect. After him again two more were dispatched in an instant. But I was the eighth. Now as soon as (with trembling) I stepped up, my companion who already sat by in his velvet, looked friendly upon me, and the Virgin her self smiled a little. But for as much as I out-stayed all the weights, the Virgin commanded them to draw me up by force, wherefore three men moreover hung on the other side of the beam, and yet could nothing prevail. Whereupon one of the Pages immediately stood up, and cried out exceeding loud, THAT IS HE. Upon which the other replied, Then let him gain his liberty, which the Virgin accorded; and being received with due ceremonies, the choice was given me to release one of the captives, whosoever I pleased; whereupon I made no long deliberation, but elected the first emperor whom I had long pittied, who was immediately set free, and with all respect seated amongst us. Now the last being set up, and the weights proving too heavy for him, in the mean while the Virgin espied my roses, which I had taken out of my hat into my hands, and thereupon presently by her Page graciously requested them of me, which I readily sent her. And so this first act was finished about ten in the fore-noon. Whereupon the trumpets began to sound again, which nevertheless we could not as yet see. Mean time the bands were to step aside with their prisoners, and expect the judgement. After which a council of the seven captains and us was set, and the business was propounded by the Virgin as president, who desired each one to give his opinion, how the prisoners were to be dealt with. The first opinion was that they should all be put to death, yet one more severely than another: namely those who had presumptuously intruded themselves contrary to the express conditions; others would have them kept close prisoners. Both which pleased neither the president nor me. At length by one of the emperors (the same whom I had freed) my companion, and my self the affair was brought to this point; that first of all the principal lords should with a befitting respect be led out of the castle; others might be carried out somewhat more scornfully. These would be stripped and caused to run out naked. The fourth with rods, whips or dogs, should be hunted out. Those who the day before willingly surrendered themselves, might be suffered to depart without any blame. And last of all those presumptuous ones, and they who behaved themselves so unseemly at dinner the day before, should be punished in body and life according to each man's demerit. This opinion pleased the Virgin well, and obtained the upper hand. There was moreover another dinner vouchsafed them, which they were soon acquainted with. But the execution was deferred till twelve at noon. Herewith the senate arose, and the Virgin also, together with her attendants returned to her usual quarter. But the uppermost table in the room was allotted to us, they requesting us to take it in good part till the business were fully dispatched. And then we should be conducted to the Lord Bridegroom and the Bride, with which we were at present well content. Mean time the prisoners were again brought into the hall, and each man seated according to his quality; they were likewise enjoined to behave themselves somewhat more civilly than they had done the day before, which yet they needed not to have been admonished, for without this, they had already put up their pipes. And this I can boldly say, not with flattery, but in the love of truth, that commonly those persons who were of the highest rank, best understood how to behave themselves in so unexpected a misfortune. Their treatment was but indifferent, yet with respect, neither could they yet see their attendants, but to us they were visible, whereat I was exceeding joyful. Now although fortune had exalted us, yet we took not upon us more than the rest, advising them to be of good cheer, the event would not be so ill. Now although they would gladly have understood the sentence of us, yet we were so deeply obliged that none durst open his mouth about it. Nevertheless we comforted them as well we could, drinking with them to try if the wine might make them any thing cheerfuller. Our table was covered with red velvet, beset with drinking cups of pure silver and gold, which the rest could not behold without amazement and very great anguish. But e'er we had seated ourselves, in came the two Pages, presenting every one in the Bride-groom's behalf, the Golden Fleece with a flying lion, requesting us to wear them at the table, and as became us to observe the reputation and dignity of the order, which his majesty had now vouchsafed us, and should suddenly be ratified with suitable ceremony. This we received with profoundest submission, promising obediently to perform whatsoever his Majesty should please. Besides these, the noble Page had a schedule, wherein we were set down in order. And for my part I should not otherwise be desirous to conceal my place, if perchance it might not be interpreted to pride in me, which yet is expressly against the fourth weight. Now because our entertainment was exceedingly stately, we demanded one of the Pages, whether we might not have leave to send some choice bit to our friends and acquaintance, who making no difficulty of it, every one sent plentifully to his acquaintance by the waiters, howbeit they saw none of them; and forasmuch as they knew not whence it came, I we. my self desirous to carry somewhat to one of them, but as soon as I was risen, one of the waiters was presently at my elbow, saying he desired me to take friendly warning, for in case one of the Pages had seen it, it would have come to the King's ear, who would certainly have taken it amiss of me; but since none had observed it but himself, he purposed not to betray me, but that I ought for the time to come to have better regard to the dignity of the order. With which words the servant did really so astonish me, that for a long time after I scarce moved upon my seat, yet I returned him thanks for his faithful warning, as well as in haste and affright I was able. Soon after the drums began to beat again, to which we were already accustomed: for we well knew it was the Virgin, wherefore we prepared ourselves to receive her, who was now coming in with her usual train, upon her high seat, one of the Pages bearing before her a very tall goblet of gold, and the other a patent in parchment. Being now after a marvellous artificial manner alighted from the seat, she takes the goblet from the Page, and presents the same in the King's behalf, saying, that it was brought from his Majesty, and that in honour of him we should cause it to go round. Upon the cover of this goblet stood Fortune curiously cast in gold, who had in her hand a red flying ensign, for which cause I drunk somewhat the more sadly, as having been but too well acquainted with Fortune's way-wardness. But the Virgin as well as we, was adorned with the

Golden Fleece and lion, whence I observed, that perhaps she wan the president of the order. Wherefore we demanded of her how the order might be named? She answered that it was not yet seasonable to discover it, till the affair with the prisoners were dispatched. And therefore their eyes were still held, and what had hitherto happened to us, was to them only for an offence and scandal, although it were to be accounted as nothing, in regard of the honour that attended us. Hereupon she began to distinguish the patent which the other Page held into two different parts, out of which about thus much was read before the first company.

That they should confess that they had too lightly given credit to fictitious books, had assumed too much to themselves, and so came into this castle, albeit they were never invited into it, and perhaps the most part had presented themselves with design to make their market here, and afterwards to live in the greater pride and lordliness; and thus one had seduced another, and plunged him into this disgrace and ignominy, wherefore they were deservedly to be soundly punished. Which they with great humility readily acknowledged, and gave their hands upon it. After which a severe check was given to the rest, much to this purpose.

That they very well knew, and were in their consciences convinced, that they had forged false fictitious books, had befooled others, and cheated them, and thereby had diminished regal dignity amongst all. They knew in like manner what ungodly deceitful figures they had made use of, in so much a. they spared not even the Divine Trinity. But accustomed themselves to cheat people the country over. It was also now as clear as day with what practices they had endeavoured to ensnare the true guests, and introduce the ignorant: in like manner, that it was manifest to all the world, that they wallowed in open whoredom, adultery, gluttony, and other uncleannesses. All which was against the express orders of our kingdom. In brief, they knew they had disparaged kingly majesty, even amongst the common sort, and therefore they should confess themselves to be manifest convicted vagabond-cheaters, knaves and rascals, whereby they deserved to be cashiered from the company of civil people, and severely to be punished.

The good artists were loath to come to this confession, but inasmuch as not only the Virgin her self threatened, and swore their death, but the other party also vehemently raged at them, and unanimously cryed out, that they had most wickedly seduced them out of the Light, they at length, to prevent a huge misfortune, confessed the same with dolour, and yet withal alledged that what had herein happened was not to be animadverted upon them in the worst sense. For in as much as the lords were absolutely resolved to get into the castle, and had promised great sums of money to that effect, each one had used all craft to seize upon something, and so things were brought to that pass, as was now manifest before their eyes. But that it succeeded not, they in their opinion had dis-deserved no more than the lords themselves; as who should have had so much understanding as to consider that in case any one had been sure of getting in, he would not, in so great peril, for the sake of a slight gain, have clambered over the wall with them. Their books also sold so mightily, that whoever had no other mean to maintain himself, was fain to engage in such a cousenage. They hoped moreover, that if a right judgment were made, they should be found no way to have miscarried, as having behaved themselves towards the lords, as became servants, upon their earnest entreaty. But answer was made them, that his Royal Majesty had determined to punish all, and every man, albeit one more severely than another. For although what had been alledged by them was partly true, and therefore the lords should not wholly be indulged, yet they had good reason to prepare themselves for death, who had so presumptuously obtruded themselves, and perhaps seduced the more ignorant against their will; as likewise they who with false books had violated royal majesty, as the same might be evinced out of their very writings and books.

Hereupon many began most pitteously to lament, cry, weep, entreat, and prostrate themselves, all which notwithstanding could avail them nothing, and I much marvelled how the Virgin could be so resolute, when yet their misery caused our eyes to run over, and moved our compassion (although the most part of them had procured us much trouble, and vexation). For she presently dispatched her Page, who brought with him all the curiassiers which had this day been appointed at the scales, who were commanded each of them to take his own to him, and in an orderly procession, so as still each curiassier should go with one of the prisoners, to conduct them into her great garden. At which time each one so exactly recognised his own man, that I marvelled at it. Leave also was likewise given to my yesterday companions to go out into the garden unbound, and to be present at the execution of the sentence. Now as soon as every man was come forth, the Virgin mounted up into her high throne, requesting us to sit down upon the steps, and to appear at the judgment, which we refused not, but left all standing upon the table (except the goblet, which the Virgin committed to the Pages keeping) and went forth in our robes upon the throne, which of it self moved so gently as if we had passed in the air, till in this manner we came into the garden, where we arose altogether. This garden was not extraordinary curious, only it pleased me that the trees were planted in so good order. Besides there ran in it a most costly fountain, adorned with wonderful figures and inscriptions, and strange characters (which God willing I shall mention in a future book). In this garden was raised a wooden scaffold, hung about with curiously painted figured coverlets. Now there were four galleries made one over another, the first more glorious than any of the rest, and therefore covered with a white taffeta curtain, so that at that time we could not perceive who-was behind it. The second was empty and uncovered. Again the two last were covered with red and blew taffeta. Now as noon as we were come to the scaffold, the Virgin bowed her self down to the ground, at which we were mightily terrified: for we might easily guess that the King and Queen must not be far off. Now we also having duely performed our reverence, the Virgin lead us up by the winding stairs into the second gallery, where she placed herself uppermost, and us in our former order. But how the emperor whom I had released, behaved himself towards me, both at this time as also before at the table, I cannot, without slander of wicked tongues, well relate. For he might well imagine in what anguish and sollicitude he now should have been, in case he were at present to attend the judgment with such ignominies and that only through me he hast not attained such dignity and worthiness. Mean time the virgin who first of all brought me the invitation, and whom hitherto I had never since seen, stepped in. First she gave one blast upon her trumpet, and then with a very loud voice declared the sentence in this manner.

The Kings Majesty my most gratious Lord could from his heart wish, that all and every one here assembled, held upon his Majesty's invitation presented themselves so qualified, as that they might (to his honour) with greatest frequently have adorned this his appointed nuptial and joyful feast. But since it hath otherwise pleased Almighty God, his Majesty hath not whereat to murmur, but must be forced, contrary to his own inclination, to abide by the ancient and laudable constitutions of this Kingdom. But now, that his Majesty's innate clemency may be celebrated over all the world, he hath thus far absolutely dealt with his council and estates, that the usual sentence shall be considerably lenified. So that in the first place he in willing to vouchsafe to the lords and potentates, not only their lives entirely, but also freely and frankly to dismiss them, friendly and courteously entreating your lordships not at all to take it in evil part that you cannot be present at his Majesty's Feast of Honour; but to remember that there in notwithstanding more imposed upon your lordship. By God Almighty (who in the distribution of his gifts hath an incomprehensible consideration) than you can duely and easily sustain. Neither is your reputation hereby prejudiced, although you be rejected by this our order, since we cannot at once all of us, do all things. But for as much as your lordships have been seduced by base rascals, it shall not on their part, pass unrevenged. And furthermore his Majesty resolveth shortly to communicate with your lordships a catalogue of hereticks or Index Expurgatorius, that you may hence forward be able with better judgment to discern between the good and the evil. And because his Majesty e're long also purposeth to rummage his library, and offer up the reductive writings to Vulcan, he friendly, humbly, and courteously entreats every one of your lordships to put the name in execution with your own, whereby it is to be hoped that all evil and mischief may for the time to come be remedied. And you are withal to be admonished, never henceforth so inconsiderately to covet an entrance hither, least the former excuse of seducers be taken from you, and you fall into disgrace and contempt of all men. In fine, for as much as the estates of the land have still somewhat to demand of your lordships, his Majesty hopes that no man will think much to redeem himself with a chain or what else he hath about him, and so in friendly manner to depart from us, and through our safe conduct to betake himself home again.

The others who stood not at the first, third and fourth weight, his Majesty will not no lightly dismiss. But that they also may now experience his Majesty's gentleness, it is his command, to strip them stark naked and so send them forth.

Those who in the second and fifth weight were found too light, shall besides stripping, be noted with one, two or more brand-marks, according as each one was lighter, or heavier.

They who were drawn up by the sixth or seventh, and not by the rest, shall be somewhat more gratiously dealt withal, and so forward. For unto every combination there was a certain punishment ordained, which were here too long to recount.

They who yesterday separated themselves freely of their own accord, shall go at liberty without any blame.

Finally, the convicted vagabond-cheaters who could move up none of the weights, shall as occasion serves, be punished in body and life, with the sword, halter, water and rods. And such execution of judgment shall be inviolably observed for an example unto others.

Herewith our Virgin broke her wand, and the other who read the sentence, blowed her trumpet, and stepped with most profound reverence towards those who stood behind the curtain. But here I cannot omit to discover somewhat to the reader concerning the number of our prisoners, of whom those who weighed one, were seven; those who weighed two, were twenty one; they who three, thirty five; they who four, thirty five; those who five, twenty one; those who six, seven; but he that came to the seventh, and yet could not well raise it, he was only one, and indeed the same whom I released. Besides, of them who wholly failed there were many. But of those who drew all the weights from the ground, but few. And these as they stood severally before us, no I diligently numbered, and noted them down in my table-book. And it is very admirable that amongst those who weighed any thing, none was equal to another. For although amongst those who weighed three, there were thirty five, yet one of them weighed the first, second, and third, another the third, fourth, and fifth, a third, the fifth, sixth and seventh and so on. It is likewise very wonderful that amongst one hundred and twenty six who weighed any thing, none was equal to another. And I would very willingly name them all, with each mans weight, were it not as yet forbidden me. But I hope it may hereafter be published with the interpretation.

Now this Judgment being read over, the lords in the first place were well satisfied, because in such severity they durst not look for a mild sentence. For which cause they gave more than they were desired, and each one redeemed himself with chains, jewels, gold, monies and other things, as much as they had about them, and with reverence took leave. Now although the King's servants were forbidden to jear any at his going away, yet some unlucky birds could not hold laughing, and certainly it was sufficiently ridiculous to see them pack away with such speed, without once looking behind them. Some desired that the promised catalogue might with the first be dispatched after them, and then they would take such order with their books as should be pleasing to his Majesty; which was again assured. At the door was given to each of them out of a cup a draught of FORGETFULNESS, that so he might have no further memory of misfortune.

After these the voluntiers departed, who because of their ingenuity were suffered to pass, but yet so as never to return again in the same fashion. But if to them (as likewise to the others) any thing further were revealed, then they should become well-come guests.

Mean while others were stripping, in which also an inequality(according to each man's demerit) was observ'd. Some were sent away naked, without other hurt. Others were driven out with small bells. Some were scourged forth. In brief the punishments were so various, that I am not able to recount them all. In the end it came to the last also with whom somewhat a longer time was spent, for whilst some were hanging, some beheading, some forced to leap into the water, and the rest otherwise dispatching, much time was consumed. Verily at this execution my eyes ran over, not indeed in regard of the punishment, which they otherwise for their impudency well deserved, but in contemplation of human blindness, in that we are continually busting ourselves in that which ever since the first Fall hath been hitherto sealed up to us. Thus the garden which so lately was quite full, was soon emptied; so that besides the soldier there was not a man left. Now as soon as this was done, and silence had been kept for the space of five minutes, there came forward a beautiful snow-white unicorn with a golden coller (having it in certain letters) about his neck. In the same place he bowed himself down upon both his fore-feet, as if hereby he had shown honour to the lion, who stood so immoveably upon the fountain, that I took him to be of stone or brass, who immediately took the naked sword which he bare in his paw, and brake it in the middle in two, the piece. whereof to my thinking sunk into the fountain: after which he so long roared, until a white dove brought a branch of olive in her bill, which the lion devoured in an instant, and so was quieted. And so the unicorn returned to his place with joy. Hereupon our Virgin lead us down again by the winding stairs from the scaffold, and so we again made our reverence toward the curtain. We were to wash our hands and heads in the fountain, and there a little while to wait in our order till the King through a certain secret gallery were again returned into his hall and then we also with choice music, pomp, state and pleasant discourse were conducted into our former lodging. And this was done about four in the afternoon. But that in the meanwhile the time might not seem too long to us, the Virgin bestowed on each of us a noble page, who were not only richly habited, but also exceedingly learned, so that they could so aptly discourse upon all subjects, that we had good reason to be ashamed of our selves. These were commanded to lead us up and down the castle yet but into certain places and if possible, to shorten the time according to our desire. Mean time the Virgin took leave with this consolation, that at supper she would be with us again, and after that celebrate the ceremonies of the hanging up of the weights, requesting that we would in patience wait till the next day, for on the morrow we must be presented to the King. She being thus departed from us, each of us did what best pleased him. One part viewed the excellent paintings, which they copied out for themselves, and considered also what the wonderful characters might signify. Others were fain to recruit themselves again with meat and drink. I indeed caused my page to conduct me (together with my companion) up and down the castle, of which walk it will never repent me as long as I have a day to live. For besides many other glorious antiquities, the royal sepulcher was also shewed me, by which I learned more than is extant in all books. There in the same place stands also the glorious Phoenix (of which two years since I published a particular small discourse) and Am resolved (in case this my narration shall prove useful) to set forth several and peculiar treatises, concerning the Lion, Eagle, Griffon, Falcon and other like, together with their draughts and inscriptions. It grieves me also for my other conforts, that they neglected such pretious treasures. And yet I cannot but think it was the special will of God it should be so. I indeed reaped the most benefit by my page, for according as each ones genius lay, so he lead his intrusted into the quarters and places which were pleasing to him. Now the keys hereunto belonging were committed to my page, and therefore this good fortune happened to me before the rest; for although he invited others to come in, yet they imagining such tombs to be only in the churchyard, thought they would well enough get thither, when ever any thing was to be seen there. Neither shall these monuments (as both of us copied and transcribed them) be withheld from my thankful scholars. The other thing that was shewed us two was the noble library as it was altogether before the Reformation. Of which (albeit it rejoices my heart as often as I call it to mind) I have so much the less to say, because the catalogue thereof in very shortly to be published. At the entry of this room stands a great book, the like whereof I never saw, in which all the figures, rooms, portals, also all the writings, riddles ant the like, to be seen in the whole castle, are delineated. Now although we made some promise concerning this also, yet at present I must contain my self, and first learn to know the world better. In every book stands its author painted, whereof (as I understood) many were to be burnt, that so even their memory may be blotted out from amongst the righteous. Now having taken a full view hereof, and being scarce gotten forth, another page came running to us, and having whispered somewhat in our pages ear, he delivered up the keys to him, who immediately carried them up the winding stair. But our page was very much out of countenance, and we setting hard upon him with entreaties, he declared to us that the King's Majesty would by no means permit that either of the two, namely the library and sepulchers, should be seen by any man and therefore he besought us as we tendered his life, to discover it to no man, he having already utterly denyed it. Whereupon both of us stood hovering between joy and fear, yet it continued in silence, and no man made further inquiry about it. Thus in both places we consumed three hours, which does not at all repent me. Now although it had already struck seven, yet nothing was hitherto given us to eat, howbeit our hunger was easie to be abated by constant revivings, and I could be well content to fast all my life long with such entertainment. About this time the curious fountains, mines, and all kind of art-shops, were also shown us, of which there was none but surpassed all our arts, though they should all be melted into one mass. All their chambers were built in semi-circle, that so they might have before their eyes the costly clock-work which was erected upon a fair turret in the center, and regulate themselves according to the course of the planets, which were to be seen on it in a glorious manner. And hence I could easily conjecture wherein our artists failed, howbeit its none of my duty to inform them. At length I came into a spacious room (shown indeed to the rest a great while before) in the middle whereof stood a terrestrial globe, whose diameter contained thirty foot, albeit near half of it, except a little which was covered with the steps, was let into the earth. Two men might readily turn this globe about with all its furniture, so that more of it was never to be seen, but so much as was above the horizon. Now although I could easily conceive that this was of some special use, yet could I not understand whereto those ringlets of gold (which were upon it in several places) served; at which my page laughed and advised me to view them more narrowly. In brief, I found there my native country noted with gold also. Whereupon my companion sought his, and found that so too. Now for as much as the same happened in like manner to the rest who stood by, the page told us of a certain that it was yesterday declared to the Kings Majest'y by their old Atlas (so is the astronomer named) that all the gilded points did exactly answer to their native countries, according as had been shown of each of them. And therefore he also, as soon as he perceived that I undervalued my self and that nevertheless there stood a point upon my native country, moved one of the captains to intreat for us, that we should be set upon the scale (without our peril) at all adventures; especially seeing one of our native countries had a notable good mark. And truly it was not without cause that he, the page who had the greatest power of all the rest, was bestowed on me. For this I then returned him thanks, and immediately looked more diligently upon my native country, and found more over that besides the ringlet, there were also certain delicate streaks upon it, which nevertheless I would not be thought to speak to my own praise or glory. I saw much more too upon this globe than I am willing to discover. Let each man take into consideration why each city produceth not a philosopher. After this he lead us quite into the globe, which was thus made. On the sea was a tablet, whereon stood three dedications, and the author's name, which a man might gently lift up and by a little joyned board, go into the center, which was capable of four persons, being nothing but a round board whereon we could sit and at ease by broad daylight (it was now already dark) contemplate the stars.

To my thinking they were mere carbuncles which glittered in an agreeable order, and moved so gallantly, that I had scarce any mind ever to go out again, as the page afterwards told the Virgin, with which she often twitched me. For it was already supper time, and I had so much amused my self in the globe, that I was almost the last at table; wherefore I made no longer delay, but having again put on my gown (which I had before laid aside) and stepping to the table, the waiters treated me with so much reverence and honour, that for shame I durst not look up, and so unawares permitted the Virgin, who attended me on one side, to stand, which she soon perceiving twitched me by the gown, and so led me to the table. To speak any further concerning the music, or the rest of that magnificent entertainment, I hold it needless both because it is not possible sufficently to express it, and I have above reported it according so my power. In brief, there was nothing there but art and amenity. Now after we had each to other related our employment since noon (howbeit, not a word was spoken of the library and monuments) being already merry with the wine the Virgin began thus: "My lords, I have a great contention with one of my sisters. In our chamber we have an eagle. Now we cherish him with such diligence. That each of us in desirous to be the best beloved, and upon that score have many a squabble. On a day we concluded to go both together to him, and toward whom he should show himself most friendly, hers should he properly be; this we did. And I (as commonly) bare in my hand a branch of laurel, but my sister had none. Now as soon as he espied us both, he immediately gave my sister another branch which he had in his beak, and offered at mine, which I gave him. Now each of us hereupon imagined her self to be best beloved of him. Which way am I to resolve my self?" This modest proposal of the Virgin pleased us all mighty well and each one would gladly have heard the solution, but in as much as they all looked upon me. And desired to have the beginning from me, my mind was so extremely confounded that I knew not what else to do with it but propound another in its stead. And therefore said, "Gracious Lady, your ladyships question were easily to be resolved if one thing did not perplex me. I had two companions, both which loved me exceedingly; now they being doubtful which of them was most dear to me, concluded to run to me unaware, and that he whom I should then embrace should be the right; this they did, yet one of them could not keep pace with the other, so he staid behind and wept; the other I embraced with amazement. Now when they had afterwards discovered the business to me, I knew not how to resolve myself and have hitherto let it rest in this manner, until I may find some good advice herein." The Virgin wondered at it, and well observed where about I was. Whereupon she replied, "well then let us both be quit," and then desired the solution from the rest. But I had already made them wise. Whereupon the next began thus: "In the city where I live, a virgin was lately condemned to death, but the judge being something pitiful towards her, caused it to be proclaimed that if any man desired to become the virgin's champion, he should have free leave to do it. Now she had two lovers; the one presently made himself ready, and came into the lists to expect his adversary; afterwards the other also presented himself. But coming somewhat too late, he resolved nevertheless to fight, and willingly suffer himself to be vanquished, that so the virgin's life might be preserved, which also succeeded according. Whereupon each challenged her. Now my lords instruct me, to which of them of right belongeth she "The Virgin could hold no longer, but said, I thought to have gained much information, and am my self gotten into the net but yet would gladly hear whether there be any more behind. "Yes, that there is " answered a third," a stranger adventure hath not been yet recounted than that which happened to my self. In my youth I loved a worthy maid. Now that this my love might attain its wished end, I was fain to make use of an ancient matron, who easily brought me to her. Now it happened that the maid's brethren came in upon us just as we three were together, who were in such a rage that they would have taken my life, but upon my vehement supplication, they at length forced me to swear to take each of them for a year, to my wedded wife. Now tell me my lords, should I take the old, or the young one first?" We all laughed sufficiently at this riddle, and although some of them muttered one to another thereupon, yet none would undertake to unfold it. Hereupon the fourth began; "In a certain city there dwelt an honourable lady, who was beloved of all, but especially by a young noble man, who would needs be too importunate with her; at length she gave him this determination, that in case he would, in a cold winter, lead her into a fair green garden of roses, then he should obtain, but if not, he must resolve never to see her more. The noble man travelled into all countries to find such a man as might perform this, till at length he lite upon a little old man that promised to do it for him, in case he would assure him of half his estate, which he having consented to the other was as good as his word. Whereupon he invited the aforesaid lady to his garden, where contrary to her expectation, she found all things green, pleasant and warm, and withal remembering her promise, she only requested that she might once more return to her lord, to whom with sighs and tears she bewailed her lamentable condition. But for as much as he sufficiently perceived her faithfulness, he dispatched her back to her lover, who had so dearly purchased her, so that she might give him satisfaction. This husband's integrity did so mightily affect the noble man, that he thought it a sin to touch so honest a wife; so he sent her home again with honour to her lord. Now the little man perceiving such faith in both these, would not, how poor soever he were, be the least, but restored the noble man all his goods again and went his way. Now my lords, I know not which of these persons may have shown the greatest ingenuity?" Here our tongues were quite cut off. Neither would the Virgin make any other reply, but only that another should go on. Wherefore the fifth, without delay, began: "My Lords, I desire not to make long work; who hath the greater joy, he that beholdeth what he loveth, Or he that only thinketh on it?" "He that beholdeth it," said the Virgin; "Nay" answered I; hereupon arose a contest, wherefore the sixth called out, 'My lords, I am to take a wife; now I have before me a maid, a married wife, and a widow; ease me of this doubt, and I will afterwards help to order the rest." "It goes well there" replied the seventh, where a man hath his choice, but with me the case is otherwise; in my youth I loved a fair and virtuous virgin from the bottom of my heart, and she me in like manner: howbeit because of her friends denial we could not come together in wedlock. Whereupon she was married to another, yet an honest and discreet person, who maintained her honourably and with affection, until she came into the pains of child-birth, which went so hard with her that all thought she had been dead, so with much state, and great mourning she was interred. Now I thought with my self, during her life thou couldst have no part in this woman, but yet now dead as she is thou mayst embrace and kiss her sufficiently; whereupon I took my servant with me, who dug her up by night. Now having opened the coffin and locked her in my arms, and feeling about her heart, I found still some little motion in it, which increased more and more from my warmth, till at last I perceived that she was indeed still alive; wherefore I quietly bare her home. and after I had warmed her chilled body with a costly bath of herbs, I committed her to my mother until she brought forth a fair son, whom (as the mother) I caused faithfully to be nursed. After two days (she being then in a mighty amazement) I discovered to her all the forepassed affair, requesting her that for the time to come she would live with me as a wife, against which she thus excepted, in case it should be grievous to her husband who had well and honourably maintained her. But if it could otherwise be, she was the present obliged in love to one as well as the other. Now after two months (being then to make a journey elsewhere) I invited her husband as a guest, and amongst other things demanded of him, whether if his deceased wife should come home again, he could be content to receive her, and he affirming it with tears and lamentations, at length I brought him his wife together with his son, and an account of all the forepassed business, intreating him to ratifie with his consent my fore-purposed espousals. After a long dispute he could not beat me from my right, but was fain to leave me the wife. But still the contest was about the son." Here the Virgin interrupted him, and said, "It makes me wonder how you could double the afflicted mans grief." "How' answered he, 'was I not then concerned?" Upon this there arose a dispute amongst us, yet the most part affirmed that he had done but right. "Nay," said he, "I freely returned him both his wife and son. Now tell me my lords, was my honesty, or this man's joy the greater? "These words had so mightily cheered the Virgin that (as if it had been for the sake or these two) she caused a health to go round. After which the rest of the proposals went on somewhat perplexedly, so that I could not retain them all, yet this comes to my mind, that one said, that a few years before he had seen a physician, who bought a parcel of wood against winter, with which he warmed himself all winter long; but as soon as the spring returned he sold the very same wood again, and so had the use of it for nothing. "Here must needs be skill," said the Virgin, "but the time is now past." "Yea," replied my companion, who ever understands not how to resolve all the riddles, may give each man notice of it by a proper messenger, I conceive he will not be denied." At this time they began to say grace, and we arose altogether from the table, rather satisfied and merry than glutted; and it were to be wished that all invitations and feastings were thus to be kept. Having now taken some few turns up and down the hall again, the Virgin asked us whether we desired to begin the wedding. "Yes," said one, noble and virtuous lady; whereupon she privately dispatched a page, and yet in the mean time proceeded in discourse with us. In brief she was already become so familiar with us, that I adventured and requested her Name. The Virgin smiled at my curiosity, but yet was not moved, but replied:

My Name contains five and fifty, and yet hath only eight letters; the third is the third part of the fifth, which added to the sixth will produce a number whose root shall exceed the third itself by just the first, and it is the half of the fourth. Now the fifth and the seventh are equal, the last and the first are also equal, and make with the second as much as the sixth hath, which contains just four more than the third tripled. Now tell me, my lord, how am I called?

The answer was intricate enough to me, yet I left not off so, but said, noble and virtuous lady, may I not obtain one only letter? Yea, said she, that may well be done. What then (replied I again) may the seventh contain? It contains (said she) as many as there are lords here. With this I was content, and easily found her Name, at which she was well pleased, with assurance that much more should yet be revealed to us. Mean time certain virgins had made themselves ready, and came in with great ceremony. First of all two youths carried lights before them; one of them was of jocund countenance, sprightly eyes and gentile proportion. The other looks something angerly, and whatever he would have, must be, as I afterwards perceived. After them first followed four virgins. One looked shame-facedly towards the earth, very humble in behaviour. The second also was a modest, bashful virgin. The third, as she entered the room seemed amazed at somewhat, and as I understood, she cannot well abide where there is too much mirth. The fourth brought with her certain small wreaths, thereby to manifest her kindness and liberality. After these four came two which were somewhat more gloriously apparelled; they saluted us courteously. One of them had a gown of sky colour spangled with golden stars. The others was green, beautified with red and white stripes. On their heads they had thin flying tissaties, which did most becomingly adorn them. At last came one alone, who had on her head a coronet, but rather looked up towards heaven, than towards earth. We all thought it had been the Bride, but were much mistaken, although otherwise in honour, riches and state she much surpassed the Bride; and she afterwards ruled the whole Wedding. Now on this occasion we all followed our Virgin, and fell down on our knees, howbeit she showed her self extreme humble, offering every one her hand, and admonishing us not to be too much surprised at this, for this was one of her smallest bounties, but to lift up our eye to our Creator, and learn hereby to acknowledge his omnipotency, and so proceed in our enterprised course, employing this grace to the praise to God, and the good of man. In sum, her words were quite different from those of our Virgin, who was somewhat more worldly. They pierced even through my bones and marrow. "And thou 'said she further to me, "hast received more than others, see that thou also make a larger return." This to me was a very strange sermon; for as soon a. we saw the virgins with the music, we imagined we must presently fall to dancing, but that time was not as yet come. Now the weights, whereof mention has been before made, stood still in the same place, wherefore the Queen (I yet knew not who she was) commanded each virgin to take up one, but to our Virgin she gave her own, which was the last and greatest, and commanded us to follow behind. Our majesty was then somewhat abated, for I well observed that our Virgin was but too good for us, and we were not so highly reputed as we our selves wore almost in part willing to fantasy. So we went behind in our order, and were brought into the first chamber, where our Virgin in the first place hung up the

Queen's weight, during which an excellent spiritual hymn was sung. There was nothing costly in this room save only curious little prayer books which should never be missing. In the midst was erected a pulpit, very convenient for prayer, where in the Queen kneeled down, and about her we were all fain to kneel and pray after the Virgin, who read out of a book, that this Wedding might tend to the honour of God, and our own benefit. Afterwards we came into the second chamber, where the first Virgin hung up her weight also, and so forward until all the ceremonies were finished. Hereupon the Queen again presented her hand to every one, and departed thence with her virgin. Our president stayed yet a while with us. But because it had been already two hours night, she would no longer detain us; me thought she was glad of our company, yet she bid us good night, and wished us quiet rest, and so departed friendly, although unwillingly from us. Our pages were well instructed in their business, and therefore showed every man his chamber, and stayed also with us in another pallet. that in case we wanted any thing we might make use of them My chamber (of the rest I am not able to speak) was royally furnished with rare tapestries and hung about with paintings. But above all things I delighted in my page, who was so excellently spoken. and experienced in the arts, that he yet spent another hour with me and it was half an hour after three when first I fell asleep. And this indeed was the first night that I slept in quiet, and yet a scurvy dream would not suffer me to rest; for I was all the night troubled with a door which I could not get open. but at last I did it. With these fantasies I passed the time. till at length cowards day I awaked.

THE FOURTH DAY

I still lay in my bed, and leisurely surveyed the noble images and figures up and down about my chamber, during which on a sudden I heard the music of coronets, as if they had been already in procession. My page skipped out of the bed as if he had been at his wits end, and looked more like one dead than living. In what case I was then, is easily imaginable, for, said he, "The rest are already presented to the King." I knew not what else to do, but weep out-right and curs s my own slothfulness; yet I dressed my self, but my page was ready long before me, and ran out of the chamber to see how affairs might yet stand. But he soon returned, and brought with him this joyful news, that the time indeed was not yet but only I had over-slept my breakfast, they being unwilling to waken me because of my age. But that now it was time for me to go with him to the fountain where the most part were assembled. With this consolation my spirit returned again, wherefore I was soon ready with my habit, and went after the page to the fountain in the aforementioned garden, where I found that the lion instead of his sword had a pretty large tablet by him. Now having well viewed it, I found that it was taken out of the ancient monuments, and placed here for some especial honour. The inscription was somewhat worn out with age, and therefore I am minded to set it down here. as it is, and give every one leave to consider it.

HERMES PRINCEPS.
POST TOT ILLATA
GENERI HUMANO DAMNA,
DEI CONSILIO:
ARTISQUE ADMINICULO,
MEDICINA SALUBRIS FACTUR
HEIC FLUO
Bibat ex me qui potest: lavet, qui vult: turbet qui audet:
BIBITE FRATRES, ET VIVITE.

(I, Hermes the Prince. After so much injury done to the human race. Through Divine Council. And through the help of the arts .Made into whoesome medicine Flow here. Drink form me who can. wash in me who likes. trouble me who dares. Drink brothers and live.)

This writing might well be read and understood, and may therefore fitly be here placed, because easier than any of the rest. Now after we had first washed our selves out of the fountain, and every man had taken a draught out of an entirely golden cup, we were once again to follow the Virgin into the hall, and there put on new apparel, which was all of cloth of gold gloriously set out with flowers. There was also given to every one another Golden Fleece, which was set about with precious stones, and various workmanship according to the utmost skill of each artificer. On it hung a weighty medal of gold, whereon were figured the sun and moon in opposition; but on the other side stood this poesie, The light of the moon shall be as the light of the sun, and the light of the sun shall be seven times lighter than at present. But our former jewels were rayed in a little casket, and committed to one of the waiters. After this the Virgin lead us out in our order, where the musicians waited ready at the door, all apparelled in red velvet with white guards. After which a door (which I never saw open before) to the Royal winding-stairs was unlocked. There the Virgin led us together with the music, up three hundred and sixty five stairs; there we saw nothing but what was of extreme costly and artificial workmanship; and still the further we went, the more glorious still was the furniture, until at length at the top we came under a painted arch, where the sixty virgins attended us, all richly apparelled. Now as soon as they had bowed to us, and we as well as we could, had returned our reverence, our musicians were dispatched away, who fain to go down the stairs again, the door being shut after them. After this a little bell was tolled; then came in a beautiful Virgin who brought every one a wreath of laurel. But our virgins had branches given them. Mean while a curtain was drawn up, where I saw the King and Queen as they sate there in their majesty, and had not the yesterday queen so faithfully warned me, I should have forgotten my self, and have equalled this unspeakable glory to Heaven.

For besides that the room glistered of mere gold and precious stones; the Queen's robes were moreover so made that I was not able to behold them. And whereas I before esteemed any thing for handsome, here all things so much surpassed the rest, as the stars in heaven are elevated.

In the mean time the Virgin steps in, and so each of the virgins taking one of us by the hand, with most profound reverence presented us to the King, whereupon the Virgin began thus to speak: "That to honour your Royal Majesties (most gracious King and Queen) these lords here present have ventured hither with peril of body and life, your Majesties have reason to rejoice, especially since the greatest part are qualified for the enlarging of your Majesties Estates and Empire, as you will find the same by a most gracious and particular examination of each of them.

Herewith I was desirous to have them in humility presented to your Majesties, with most humble suit to discharge me of this my commission, and most graciously to take sufficient information from each or them, concerning both my actions and omissions." Hereupon she laid down her branch upon the ground. Now it would have been very fitting for one of us to have put in and spoken somewhat on this occasion, but seeing we were all troubled with the falling of the uvula, at length the old Atlas steps forward and spoke on the King's behalf; "Their Royal Majesties do most graciously rejoice at your arrival, and will that their Royal Grace be assured to all, and every man. And with thy administration, gentle Virgin, they are most graciously satisfied, and accordingly a Royal Reward shall therefore be provided for thee. Yet it is still their intention, that thou shalt this day also continue with them, in as much as they have no reason to mistrust thee." Hereupon the Virgin humbly took up the branch again. And so we for the first time were to step aside with our Virgin. This room was square on the front, five times broader than it was long; but towards the West it had a great arch like a porch, wherein in circle stood three glorious royal thrones, yet the middle-most was somewhat higher than the rest. Now in each throne sate two persons. In the first sate a very antient King with a grey beard, yet his consort was extraordinarily fair and young. In the third throne sate a black King of middle age, and by him a dainty old matron, not crowned, but covered with a vail. But in the middle sate the two young persons, who tho' they had likewise wreaths of laurel upon their heads, yet over them hung a large and costly crown. Now albeit they were not at this time so fair as I had before imagined to my self, yet so it was to be. Behind them on a round form sat for the most part antient men, yet none of them (at which I wondered) had any sword, or other weapon about him. Neither saw I any other life-guard, but certain Virgins which were with us the day before, who sate on the sides of the arch. Here can I not pass in silence how the little Cupid flew to and again there, but for the most part he hovered and played the wanton about the great crown; sometimes he seated himself between the two lovers, somewhat smiling upon them with his bow. Nay, sometimes he made as if he would shoot one of us. In brief, this knave was so full of his waggery, that he would not spare even the little birds, which in multitudes flew up and down the room, but tormented them all he could.

The virgins had also their pastimes with him, but whensoever they could catch him, it was not so easy a matter for him to get from them again. Thus this little knave made all the sport and mirth. Before the Queen stood a small, but unpressibly curious altar, wherein lay a book covered with black velvet, only a little over-rayed with gold. By this stood a small taper in an ivory candlestick. Now although it were very small, yet it burnt continuously, and stood in that manner, that had not Cupid, in sport, now and then puffed upon it, we could not have conceived it to be fire. By this stood a sphere or celestial globe, which of itself turned clearly about. Next this, a small striking-watch, by that a little christal pipe or siphon-fountain, out of which perpetually ran a clear blood-red liquor; and last of all a skull, or death's head; in this was a white serpent, which was of such a length, that though she crept circle-wise about the rest of it, yet her taile still remained in one of the eye-holes, until her head again entered at the other, so she never stirred from her skull, unless it happened that Cupid twitched a little at her, for then she slips in so suddenly, that we all could not choose but marvel at it. Together with this altar, there were up and down the room wonderful images, which moved themselves, as if they had been alive, and had so strange a contrivance, that it would be impossible for me to relate it all. Likewise, as we were passing out, there began such a marvellous kind of vocal music, that I could not certainly tell, whether it were performed by the virgins who yet stayed behind, or by the images themselves. Now we beeing for this time satisfied, went thence with our virgins, who, the musicians being already present, led us down the winding stairs again, but the door was diligently locked and bolted. As soon as we were come again into the hall, one of the virgins began: "I wonder, Sister, that you dourest adventure your self amongst so many persons." My Sister," replied our president, "I am fearful of none so much as of this man," pointing at me. This speech went to the heart of me, for I well understood that she mocked at my age, and indeed I wan the oldest of them all. Yet she comforted me again with promise, that in case I behaved my self well towards her, she would easily rid me of this burden. Mean time a collation was again brought in, and every one's virgin seated by him, who well knew how to shorten the time with handsome discourses, but what their discourses and sports were I dare not blab out of school. But most of the questions were about the arts, whereby I could lightly gather that both young and old were conversant in the sciences. But still it run in my thoughts how I might become young again, whereupon I wan somewhat the sadder. This the Virgin perceived, and therefore began, "I dare lay anything, if I lye with him to night, he shall be pleasanter in the morning." Hereupon they began to laugh, and albeit I blushed all over, yet I was fain to laugh too at my own ill-luck. Now there was one there that had a mind to return my disgrace again upon the Virgin, whereupon he said, "I hope not only we, but the virgins too themselves will bear witness in behalf of our brother, that our lady president hath promised her self to be his bedfellow to night." "I should be well content with it," replied the Virgin, "if I had no reason to be afraid of these my sisters; there would be no hold with them should I choose the best and handsomest for my self, against their will." My Sister presently began another, "we find hereby that thy high office makes thee not proud; wherefore if by thy permission we might by lot part the lords here present, amongst us, for bed-fellows, thou shouldst with our good will have such a prerogative." We let this pass for a jeast, and began again to discourse together. But our Virgin could not leave tormenting us, and therefore began again, "My lords, how if we should permit fortune to decide which of us must lie together to night? "Well," said I, "if it may be no otherwise, we cannot refuse such a proffer." Now because it was concluded to make this trial after meat, we resolved to sit no longer at table, so we arose, and each one walked up and down with his virgin. "Nay," said the Virgin, "it shall not be so yet, but let us see how fortune will couple us," upon which we were separated asunder. But now first arose a dispute how the business should be carried, but this was only a premeditated device, for the Virgin instantly made the proposal that we should mix our selves together in a ring, and that she beginning to count from her self, the seventh, was to be content with the following seventh, whether it were a virgin, or man. For our parts we were not aware of any craft, and therefore permitted it so to be; but when we thought we had very well mingled our selves, the virgins nevertheless were so subtle, that each one knew her station beforehand. The Virgin began to reckon, the seventh next her was again a virgin, the third seventh a virgin likewise, and this happened so long till (to our amazement) all the virgins came forth, and none of us was hit. Thus we poor pitiful wretches remained standing alone, and were moreover forced to suffer our selves to be jeared too. and confess we were very handsomely couzened. In short, who ever had seen us in our order, might sooner have expected the skye to fall, then that it should never have come to our turn. Herewith our sport was at an end, and we were fain to satisfy our selves with the Virgin's . In the interim, the little wanton Cupid came also in unto us. But because he presented himself on behalf of their Royal Majesties, and delivered us a health (as from them) out of a golden cup, and was to call our virgins to the King, withal declaring he could at this time tarry no longer with them, we could not sufficiently sport our selves with him. So with a due return of our most humble thanks we let him fly forth again. Now because (in the interim) the mirth began to fall into my consort's feet. and the virgins were nothing sorry to see it, they quickly lead up a civil dance, whom I rather beheld with pleasure then assisted, for my mercurialists were so ready with their postures, as if they had been long of the trade. After some few dances our president came in again, and told us how the artists and students had offered themselves to their Royal Majesties, for their honour and pleasure. before their departure to act a merry comedy; and if we thought good to be present at it, and to wait upon their Royal Majesties to the House of the Sun, it would be acceptable to them, and they would most gratiously acknowledge it. Hereupon in the first place we returned our most humble thanks for the honour vouchsafed us; not only so, but moreover most submissively tendered our small service which the Virgin related again, and presently brought word to attend their Royal Majesties (in our order) in the gallery, whither we were soon led, and stayed not long there; for the Royal Procession was just ready, yet without any music at all. The unknown Queen who was yesterday with us, went foremost. with a small and costly coronet, apparelled in white satin, she carried nothing but a small crucifix which was made of a pearl, and this very day wrought between the young King and his Bride. After her went the six fore-mentioned virgins in two ranks, who carried the King's jewels belonging to the little altar. Next to these came the three Kings. The Bridegroom was in the midst of them in a plain dress, only in black satin, after the Italian mode. He had on a small round black hat, with a little black pointed feather, which he courteously put off to us, thereby to signify his favour towards us. To him we bowed our selves, as also to the first, as we had been before instructed. After the Kings came the three Queens, two whereof were richly habited, only she in the middle went likewise all in black, and Cupid held up her train. After this, intimation was given to us to follow, and after us the virgins, till at last old Atlas brought up the rear. In such procession, through many stately walks, we at length came to the House of the Sun, there next to the King and Queen, upon a richly furnished scaffold, to behold the fore-ordained comedy. We indeed, though separated, stood on the right hand of the Kings, but the virgins on the left, except those to whom the Royal Ensigns were committed. To them was allotted a peculiar standing at top of all. But the rest of the attendants were fain to stand below between the columns, and therewith to be content. Now because there are many remarkable passages in this comedy, I will not omit in brief to run it over.

First of all came forth a very ancient King. with some servants, before whose throne was brought a little chest, with mention that it was found upon the water. Now it being opened, there appeared in it a lovely babe, together with certain jewels, and a small letter of parchment sealed and superscribed to the King, which the King therefore presently opened, and having read it, wept, and then declared to his servants how injuriously the King of the Moors had deprived his aunt of her country, and had extinguished all the royal seed even to his infant, with the daughter of which country he had now purposed to have matched his son. Hereupon he swore to maintain perpetual enmity with the Moor and his allies, and to revenge this upon him; and therewith commanded that the child should be tenderly nursed, and to make preparation against the Moor. Now this provision and the discipline of the young lady (who after she was a little grown up was committed to an ancient tutor) continued all the first act, with many very fine and laudable sports besides.

In the interlude a lion and griffon were set at one another, to fight, and the lion got the victory, which was also a pretty sight.

In the second act, the Moor, a very black treacherous fellow, came forth also; who having with vexation understood that his murder was discovered, and that too a little lady was craftily stolen from him, began thereupon to consult how by stratagem he might be able to encounter so powerful an adversary, whereof he was at length advised by certain fugitives who by reason of famine fled to him. So the young lady contrary to all men's expectation, fell again into his hands, whom, had he not been wonderfully deceived by his own servants, he had like to have caused to be slain. Thus this act too was concluded with a marvellous triumph of the Moor.

In the third act a great army on the King's party was raised against the Moor, and put under the conduct of an ancient valiant knight, who fell into the Moors country, till at length he forceably rescued the young lady out of the tower, and apparelled her a new. After this in a trice they erected a glorious scaffold, and placed their young lady upon it. Presently came twelve royal ambassadors, amongst whom the fore-mentioned knight made a speech, alleging that the King his most gracious lord had not only heretofore delivered her from death, and even hitherto caused her to be royally brought up (though she had not behaved her self altogether as became her), but moreover his Royal Majesty had, before others, elected her, to be a spouse for the young lord his son, and most graciously desired that the said espousals might be really executed in case they would be sworn to his Majesty upon the following articles. Hereupon out of a patent he caused certain glorious conditions to be read. which if it were not too long, were well worthy to be here recounted. In brief, the young lady took an oath inviolably to observe the same, returning thanks withal in most seemly sort for this so high a grace. Whereupon they began to sing to the praise of God, of the King, and the young lady, and so for this time departed. For sport, in the mean while, the four beasts of Daniel, as he saw them in the vision, and hath at large described them, were brought in, all which had its certain signification.

In the fourth act the young lady was again restored to her lost kingdom, and crowned, and for a space, in this array, conducted about the place with extraordinary joy. After this many and various ambassadors presented themselves, not only to wish her prosperity, but also to behold her glory. Yet it was not long that she preserved her integrity, but soon began again to look wantonly about her, and to wink at the ambassadors and lords, wherein she truly acted her part to the life.

These her manners were soon known to the Moor, who would by no means neglect such an opportunity, and because her steward had not sufficient regard to her, she was easily blinded with great promises, so that she had no good confidence in her King but privily submitted her self to the entire disposal of the Moor. Hereupon the; Moor made haste, and having (by her consent) gotten her into his hands, he gave her good words so long till all her kingdom had subjected itself to him, after which in the third scene of this act, he caused her to be led forth, and first to be strips stark naked, and then upon a scurvy wooden scaffold to be bound to a post, and well scourged, and at last sentenced to death. This was so woeful a spectacle, that it made the eyes of many to run over. Hereupon thus naked as she was, she was cast into prison, there to expect her death, which was to be procured by poison, which yet killed her not but made her leprous all over. Thus this act was for the most part lamentable.

Between, they brought forth Nebuchadnezzar's image, which was adorn 'd with all manner of arms, on the head, breast, belly, legs and feet, and the like, of which too more shall be spoken in the future explication.

In the fifth act the young King was acquainted with all that had passed between the Moor and his future spouse, who first interceeded with his father for her, intreating that she might not be left in that condition; which his father having agreed to, ambassadors were dispatched to comfort her in her sickness and captivity, but yet withal to give her notice of her inconsiderateness. But she would not yet receive them, but consented to be the Moor's concubine, which was also done, and the young King was acquainted with it.

After this comes a band of fools, each of which brought with him a cudgel, where within a trice they made a great globe of the world, and soon undid it again. It was fine sportive fantasy.

In the sixth act the young King resolved to bid battle to the Moor, which also was done. And albeit the Moor was discomfited, yet all held the young King too for dead. At length he came to himself again, released his spouse, and committed her to his steward and chaplain, the first whereof tormented her mightily; at last the leaf turned over, and the priest was so insolently wicked, that he would needs be above all, until the same was reported to the young King, who hastily dispatched one who broke the neck of the priest's mightiness, and adorned the bride in some measure for the nuptials.

After the act a vast artificial elephant was brought forth. He carries a great tower with musicians, which was also well pleasing to all.

In the last act the bride-groom appeared in such pomp as is not well to be believed, and was amazed how it was brought to pass. The bride met him in the like solemnity, whereupon all the people cried out VIVAT SPONSUS, VIVAT SPONSA (Long live the bridegroom, Long live the bride.) so that by this comedy they did withal congratulate our King and Queen in the most stately manner, which (as I well observed) pleased them most extraordinarily well.

At length they made some paces about the stage in such procession, till at last they altogether they began thus to sing.

I

This time full of love
Does our Joy much improve
Because of the King's nuptial;
And therefore let's sing
That from all parts it ring,
Blest be he that granted us all.

II

The Bride most exquisitely fair,
Whom we attended with long care
To him in troth's now plighted:
We fully have at length obtained
The same for which we did contend:
He's happy, that's fore-sighted.

III

Now the parents kind and good
By intreaties are subdu'd:
Long enough in hold was she mew'd;
In honour increase,
Till thousands arise
And spring from your own proper blood.

After this thanks were returned, and the comedy was finished with joy, and the particular good liking of the Royal Persons wherefore (the evening also being already hard by) they departed together in their fore-mentioned order. But we were to attend the Royal Persons up the winding stairs into the forementioned hall, where the tables were already richly furnished, and this was the first time that we were invited to the Kings table. The little altar was placed in the midst of the hall, and the six fore-named royal ensigns were laid upon it. At this time the young King behaved himself very gratiously towards us, but yet he could not be heartily merry. But howbeit he now and then discoursed a little with us, yet he often sighed, at which the little Cupid only mocked, and played his waggish tricks. The old King and Queen were very serious, only the wife of one of the ancient Kings was gay enough, the cause of which I yet understood not. During this, the Royal Persons took up the first table, at the second we only sate. At the third, some of the principal virgins placed themselves. The rest of the virgins, and men, were all fain to wait. This was performed with such state and solemn stillness, that I am afraid to make many words of it. Here I cannot leave untouched how that all the Royal Persons, before meat, attired themselves in snow-white glittering garments, and so sate down to table. Over the table hung the great golden crown, the precious stones whereof, without any other light, would have sufficiently illuminated the hall. However all the lights were kindled at the small taper upon the altar; what the reason was I did not certainly know. But this I took very good notice of, that the young King frequently sent meat to the white serpent upon the little altar, which caused me to muse. Almost all the prattle at this banquet was made by little Cupid, who could not leave us (and me indeed especially) untormented. He was perpetually producing some strange matter. However, there was no considerable mirth, all went silently on, from whence I, by my self, could imagine some great imminent peril. For there was no music at all heard; but if we were demanded any thing, we were fain to give short round answers, and so let it rest. In short, all things had so strange a face, that the sweat began to trickle down all over my body; and I am apt to believe that the stoutheartedst man alive would then have lost his courage. Supper being now almost ended, the young King commanded the book to be reached him from the little altar. This he opened, and caused it once again by an old man to be propounded to us, whether we resolved to abide with him in prosperity and adversity; which we having with trembling consented to, he further caused us sadly to be demanded, whether we would give him our hands on it, which, when we could find no evasion, was fain so to be. Hereupon one after another arose, and with his own hand writ himself down in this book. When thin also was performed, the little crystal fountain, together with a very small crystal glass was brought near, out of which all the Royal Person, one after another drank, Afterwards it was reached to us too, and so forward to all persons, and this was called, the Draught of Silence. Hereupon all the Royal Persons presented us their hands, declaring that in case we did not now stick to them, we should now and never more hereafter see them; which verily made our eyes run over. But our president engaged her self and promised very largely on our behalf, which gave them satisfaction. Mean time a little bell was tolled, at which all the Royal Persons waxed so mighty bleak, that we were ready utterly to despair. They quickly put off their white garments again, and put on entirely black ones. The whole hall likewise was hung about with black velvet, the floor we covered with black velvet, with which also the ceiling above (all this being before prepared) was overspread. After that the tables were also removed away, had all had seated themselves round about upon the form, and we also had put on black habits. In comes our president again, who was before gone out, and brought with her six black taffeta scarffs, with which she bound the six Royal Persona eyes. Now when they could no longer see, there were immediately brought in by the servants six covered coffins, and set down in the hall also a low black seat placed in the midst. Finally, there steps in a very coal-black tall man, who bare in his hand a sharp axe. Now after that the old King hat been first brought to the seat, his head was instantly whips off, and wrapped up in a black cloth, but the blood was received into a great golden goblet, had placed with him in this coffin that stood by, which being covered was set aside. Thus it went with the rest also, so that I thought it would at length have come to me too, but it did not. For as noon as the six Royal Persons were beheaded, the black man went out again; after whom another followed, who beheaded him too just before the door, and brought back his head together with the axe, which were laid in a little chest. This indeed to me seemed a bloody Wedding, but because I could not tell what would yet be the event, I was fain for that time to captivate my understanding until I were further resolved.

For the Virgin too, seeing that some of us were faint-hearted and wept, bid us be content. For, said she to us, "The life of these standeth now in your hands, and in case you follow me, this death shall make many alive." Herewith she intimated we should go sleep, and trouble our selves no further on our part, for they should be sure to have their due right. And so she bad us all good night, saying that she must watch the dead corps this night. We did so, and were each of us conducted by our pages into our lodgings. My page talked with me of sundry and various matters (which I still very well remember) and gave me cause enough to admire at his Understanding. But his intention was to lull me asleep, which at last I well observed, whereupon I made as though I was fast asleep, but no sleep came into my eyes, and I could not put the beheaded out of my mind. Now my lodging was directly over against the great lake, no that I could well look upon it, the windows being nigh the bed. About midnight, as soon as it had struck twelve, on a sudden I espied on the lake a great fire, wherefore out of fear I quickly opened the window to nee what would become of it. Then from far I saw seven ships making forward, which were all stuck full of lights. Above on the top of each of them hovered a flame that passed to and fro, and sometimes descended quite down, as that I could lightly Judge that it must needs be the spirits of the beheaded. Now these ships gently approached to land, and each of them had no more than one mariner. As soon as they were now gotten to shore, I presently espied our Virgin with a torch going towards the ship, after whom the six covered coffins, together with the little chest, were carried, and each of them privily laid in a ship. Wherefore I awakened my page too, who hugely thanked me, for having run much up and down all the day, he might quite have overslept this, tho' he well knew it. Now as soon as the coffins were laid in the ships, all the lights were extinguished, and the six flames passed back together over the lake so that there was no more but one light in each ship for a watch. There were also some hundreds of watchmen who had encamped themselves on the shore, and sent the Virgin back again into the castle, who carefully bolted all up again, so that I could well judge that there was nothing more to be done this night, but that we must expect the day, so we again betook ourselves to rest. And I only of all my company had a chamber towards the lake, and saw this, so that now I was also extreme weary, and so fell asleep in my manifold speculations.

THE FIFTH DAY

The night was over, and the dear wished for day broken, when hastily I got me out of bed, more desirous to learn what might yet ensue, than that I had sufficiently slept. Now after that I had put on my clothes, and according to my custom was gone down the stairs, it was still too early, and I found nobody else in the hall, wherefore I entreated my page to lead me a little about the castle, and show me somewhat that was rare, who was now (as always) willing, and presently lead me down certain steps underground, to a great iron door, on which the following words in great copper letters were fixed:

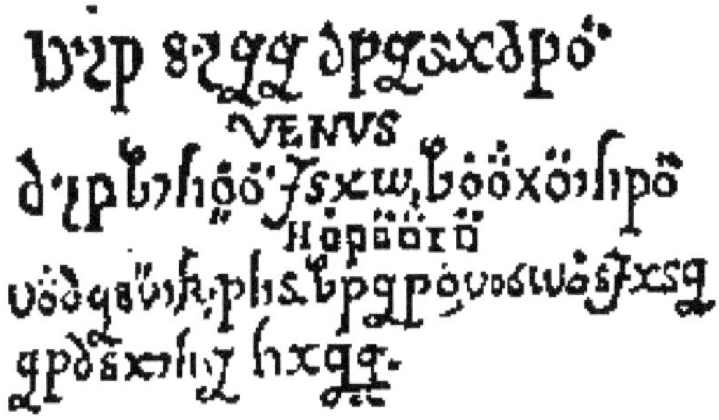

[decorative script text:]
VENUS
Hopooto

This I thus copied, and set down in my table-book. Now after this door was opened, the page led me by the hand through a very dark passage, till we came again to a very little door, that was now only put too, for (as my page informed me) it was first opened but yesterday when the coffins were taken out, and had not been since shut. Now as soon as we stepped in, I espied the most precious thing that Nature ever created, for this vault had no other light but from certain huge great carbuncles, and this (as I was informed) was the King's Treasury. But the most glorious and principal thing, that I here saw, was a sepulchre (which stood in the middle) so rich that I wondered that it was no better guarded, whereunto the page answered me, that I had good reason to be thankful to my planet, by whose influence it was that I had now seen certain pieces which no humane eye else (except the King's family) had ever had a view of. This sepulchre was triangular, and had in the middle of it a kettle of polished copper, the rest was of pure gold and precious stones. In the kettle stood an angel, who held in his arms an unknown tree, from which it continually dropped fruit into the kettle; and an oft as the fruit fell into the kettle, it turned into water, and ran out from thence into three small golden kettles standing by. This little altar was supported by these three animals, an eagle, an ox and a lion, which stood on an exceeding costly base. I asked my page what this might signify. "Here," said he, "lies buried Lady Venus, that beauty which hath undone many a great man, both in fortune, honour, blessing and prosperity." After which he showed me a copper door on the pavement. "Here," said he, "if you please, we may go further down." "I still follow you," replied I. So I went down the steps, where it was exceeding dark, but the page immediately opened a little chest, wherein stood a small ever-burning taper, at which he kindled one of the many torches which lay by. I was mightily terrified, and seriously asked how he durst do this? He gave me for answer, "As long as the Royal Persons are still at rest, I have nothing to fear." Herewith I espied a rich bed ready made, hung about with-curious curtains, one of which he drew, where I saw the Lady Venus stark-naked (for he heaved up the coverlets too) lying there in such beauty, and a fashion so surprising, that I was almost besides myself, neither do I yet know whether it was a piece thus carved, or a human corpse that lay dead there. For she was altogether immovable, and yet I durst not touch her. So she was again covered, and the curtain drawn before her, yet she was still (as it were) in my eye. But I soon espied behind the bed a tablet on which it was thus written:

I asked my page concerning this writing, but he laughed, with promise that I should know it too. So he putting out the torch, we again ascended. Then I better viewed all the little doors, and first found that on every corner there burned a small taper of pyrites, of which I had before taken no notice, for the fire was so clear, that it looked much like a stone than a taper. From this heat the tree was forced continually to melt, yet it still produced new fruit. Now behold (said the page) what I heard revealed to the King by Atlas. When the tree (said he) shall be quite melted down, then shall Lady Venus awake, and be the mother of a King. Whilst he was thus speaking, in flew the little Cupid, who at first was somewhat abashed at our presence, but seeing us both look more like the dead than the living, he could not at length refrain from laughing, demanding what spirit had brought me thither, whom I with trembling answered, that I had lost my way in the castle, and was by chance come hither, and that the page likewise had been looking up and down for me, and at last lighted upon me here, I hoped he would not take it amiss. "Nay then 'tis well enough yet," said Cupid, "my old busy grandsire, but you might lightly have served me a scurvy trick, had you been aware of this door. Now I must look better to it," and so he put a strong lock on the copper door, where we before descended. I thanked God that he lighted upon us no sooner. My page too was the more jocund, because I had so well helped him at this pinch.

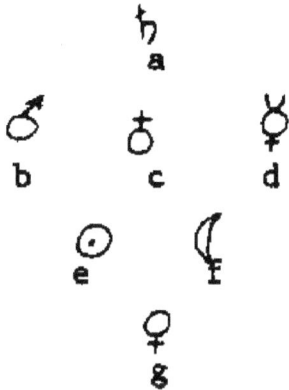

"Yet can I not," said Cupid "let it pass unrevenged, that you were so near stumbling upon my dear mother." With that he put the point of his dart into one of the little tapers, and heating it a little, pricked me with it on the hand, which at that time I little regarded, but was glad that it went so well with us, and that we came off without further danger. Meantime my companions were gotten out of bed too, and were again returned into the hall. To whom I also joined myself, making as if I were then first risen. After Cupid had carefully made all fast again, he came likewise to us, and would needs have me show him my hand, where he still found a little drop of blood, at which he heartily laughed, and bade the rest have a care of me, as I would shortly end my days. We all wondered how Cupid could be so merry, and have no sense at all of the yesterday's sad passages. But he was no what troubled. Now our president had in the mean time made herself ready for the journey, coming in all in black velvet, yet she still bare her branch of laurel. Her virgins too had their branches. Now all things being in readiness, the Virgin bid us first drink somewhat, and then presently prepare for the procession, wherefore we made no long tarrying but followed her out of the hall into the court. In the court stood six coffins, and my companions thought no other but that the six Royal Persons lay in them, but I well observed the device. Yet I knew not what was to be done with these other. By each coffin were eight muffled men. Now as soon as the music went (it was so mournful and dolesome a tune, that I was astonished at it) they took up the coffins, and we (as we were ordered) were fain to go after them into the forementioned garden, in the midst of which was erected a wooden edifice, having round about the roof a glorious crown, and standing upon seven columns; within it were formed six sepulchres, and by each of them a stone, but in the middle it had a round hollow rising stone. In these graves the coffins were quietly and with many ceremonies laid. The stones were shoved over them, and they shut fast. But the little chest was to lie in the middle. Herewith were my companions deceived, for they imagined no other but that the dead corpse were there. Upon the top of all there was a great flag, having a phoenix painted on it, perhaps therewith the more to delude us. Here I had great occasion to thank God that I had seen more than the rest. Now after the funerals were done, the Virgin, having placed her self upon the middle-most stone, made a short oration, that we should be constant to our engagements, and not repine at the pains we were hereafter to undergo, but be helpful in restoring the present buried Royal Persons to life again, and therefore without delay to rise up with her, to make a journey to the tower of Olympus, to fetch from thence medicines useful and necessary for this purpose. This we soon agreed to, and followed her through another little door guise to the shore. There the seven forementioned ships stood all empty, on which all the virgins stuck up their laurel branches, and after they had distributed us in the six ships, they caused us in Gods name thus to begin our voyage, and looked upon us as long as they could have us in sight, after which they with all the watch-men returned into the castle. Our ships had each of them a peculiar device. Five of them indeed had the five regular bodies, each a several one, but mine in which the Virgin too sat, carried a globe. Thus we sailed on in a singular order, and each had only two mariners. Foremost went the ship as in which, as I conceive the Moor lay. In this were twelve musicians, who played excellent well, and its device was a pyramid. Next followed three a breast, b, c, and d, in w hich we were disposed. I sat in c. In the midst behind these came the two fairest and stateliest ships, e and f, stuck about with many branches of laurel, having no passengers in them; their flags were the sun and moon. But in the rear only one ship g, in this were forty virgins. Now being thus passed over this lake, we first came through a narrow arm, into the right sea, where all the sirens, nymphs, and sea-goddesses had attended us; wherefore they immediately dispatched a sea-nymph to us to deliver their present and offering of honour to the Wedding. It was a costly, great, set, round and orient pearl, the like to which hath not at any time been seen, either in ours, or yet in the new world. Now the Virgin having friendly received it, the nymph further entreated that audience might be given to their divertissements, and to make a little stand, which the Virgin was content to do, and commanded the two great ships to stand into the middle, and with the rest to encompass them in pentagon. After which the nymphs fell into a ring about them, and with a most delicate sweet voice began thus to sing:

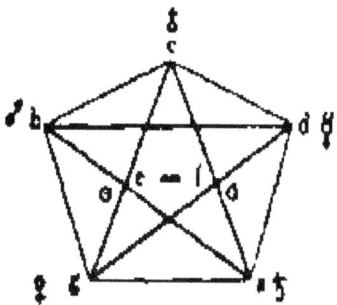

I

There's nothing better here below,
Than beauteous, noble, Love;
Whereby we like to God do grow,

And none to grief do move.
Wherefore let's chant it to the King,
That all the sea thereof may ring.
We question; answer you.

II

What was it that at first us made?
'Twas Love.
And what hath grace a fresh conveigh'd?
'Tis Love.
Whence was't (pray tell us) we were born?
Of Love
How came we then again forlorn?
Sans Love.

III

Who was it (say) that us conceived?
'Twas. Love.
Who suckled, nursed, and reliev'd?
'Twas Love.
What is it we to our parents owe?
'Tis Love.
What do they us such kindness show?
Of Love.

IV

Who get's herein the victory?
'Tis Love.
Can Love by search obtained be?
By Love.
How may a man good works perform?
Through Love.
Who into one can two transform?
'Tis Love.
V
Then let our song sound,
Till it's eccho rebound.
To Loves honour and praise,

Which may ever increase
With our noble Princes, the King,
and the Queen,
The soul is departed, their body's within.

VI

And as long as we live,
God graciously give;
That as great love and amity,
They bear each other mightily;
So we likewise, by Loves own flame,
May reconjoyn them once again.

VII

Then this annoy
Into great joy
(If many thousand younglings deign)
Shall change, and ever so remain.

They having with most admirable consent and melody finished this song, I no more wondered at Ulysses for stopping the ears of his companions, for I seemed to my self the most unhappy man alive, that nature had not made me too so trim a creature. But the Virgin soon dispatched them, and commanded to set sail from thence; wherefore the nymphs too after they had been presented with a long red scarf for a gratuity, went off, and dispersed themselves in the sea. I was at this time sensible that Cupid began to work with me too, which yet tended but very little to my credit, and for as much as my giddiness is likely to be nothing beneficial to the reader, I am resolved to let it rest as it in. But this was the very wound that in the first book I received on the head in a dream. And let every one take warning by me of loitering about Venus's bed, for Cupid can by no means brook it. After some hours, having in friendly discourses made a good way, we came within ken of the Tower of Olympus, wherefore the Virgin commanded by the discharge of some pieces to give the signal of our approach, which was also done. And immediately we espied a great white flag thrust out, and a small gilded pinnace sent forth to meet us. Now as soon as this was come to us, we perceived in it a very ancient man, the warden of the Tower, with certain guards clothed in white, of whom we were friendly received, and so conducted to the Tower. This Tower was situated upon an island exactly square, which was environed with a wall so firm and thick, that I my self counted two hundred and sixty passes over. On the other side of the wall was a fine meadow with certain little gardens, in which grew strange, and to me unknown, fruits; and then again an inner wall about the Tower. The Tower of it self was just as if seven round towers had been built one by another, yet the middlemost was somewhat the higher, and within they all entered one into another, and had seven storeys one above another. Being thus come to the gates of the Tower, we were led a little aside on the wall, that so, as I well observed, the coffins might be brought into the Tower without our taking notice; of this the rest knew nothing. This being done, we conducted into the Tower at the very bottom, which albeit it were excellently painted, yet we had here little recreation, for this was nothing but a laboratory, where we were fain to beat and wash plants, and precious stones, and all sorts of things, and extract their juice and essence, and put up the same in glasses, and deliver them to be laid up. And truly our Virgin was so busy with us, and so full of her directions, that she knew how to give each of us employment enough, so that in this island we were fain to be mere drudges, till we had achieved all that was necessary for the restoring of the beheaded bodies. Meantime (as I afterwards understood) three virgins were in the first apartment washing the corpse with all diligence. Now having at length almost done with this our preparation, nothing more was brought us, but some broth with a little draught of wine, whereby I well observed, that we were not here for our pleasure; for when we had finished our days work too, every one had only a mattress laid on the ground for him, where with we were to content ourselves. For my part I was not very much troubled with sleep, and therefore walked out into the garden, and at length came as far as the wall; and because the heaven was at that time very clear, I could well drive away the time in contemplating the stars. By chance I came to a great pair of stone stairs, which led up to the top of the wall. And because the moon shone very bright, I was so much the more confident, and went up, and looked too a little upon the sea, which was now exceeding calm; and thus having good opportunity to consider better of astronomy, I found that this present night there would happen such a conjunction of the planets, the like to which was not otherwise suddenly to be observed. Now having looked a good little into the sea, and it being just about midnight, as soon as it had struck twelve, I beheld from far the seven flames passing over sea hitherward, and betaking themselves to the top of the spire of the Tower. This made me somewhat afraid for as soon as the flames had settled themselves, the winds arose, and began to make the sea very tempestuous. The moon also was covered with clouds, and my joy ended with such fear, that I had scarce time enough to hit upon the stairs again, and betake my self again to the Tower. Now whether the flames tarried any longer, or passed away again, I cannot say, for in this obscurity I durst no more venture abroad. So I laid me down upon my mattress, and there being besides in the laboratory a pleasant and gently purling fountain, I fell asleep so much the sooner. And thus this fifth day too was concluded with wonders.

THE SIXTH DAY

Next morning, after we had awakened one another, we sat together a while to discourse what might yet be the event of things. For some were of opinion what they should all be enlivened again together. Others contradicted it, because the decease of the ancients was not only to restore life, but increase too to the young ones. Some imagined that they were not put to death, but that others were beheaded in their stead. We having now talked together a pretty long while, in comes the old man, and first saluting us, looks about him to see if all things were ready, and the processes enough done. We had herein so behaved ourselves, that he had no fault to find with our diligence, whereupon he placed all the glasses together, and put them into a case. Presently come certain youths bringing with them some ladders, ropes, and large wings, which they laid down before us, and departed. Then the old man began thus: "My dear sons, one of these three things must each of you this day constantly bear about with him. Now it is free for you either to make a choice of one of them, or to cast lots about it." We replied, we would choose. "Nay, said he, "let it rather go by lot." Hereupon he made three little schedules. On one he writ Ladder, on the second Rope, on the third Wings. These he laid in a hat, and each man must draw, and whatever he happened upon, that was to be his. Those who got the ropes, imagined themselves to be in the best case, but I chanced on a ladder, which hugely afflicted me, for it was twelve-foot long, and pretty weighty, and I must be forced to carry it, whereas the others could handsomely coil their ropes about them. And as for the wings, the old man joined them so nearly on to the third sort, as if they had grown upon them. Hereupon he turned the cock and then the fountain ran no longer, and we were fain to remove it, from the middle out of the way. After all things were carried off, he taking with him the casket with the glasses, took leave, and locked the door fast after him so that we imagined no other but that we had been imprisoned in this Tower. But it was hardly a quarter of an hour before a round hole at the very top was uncovered, where we saw our Virgin, who called to us, and bad us good morrow, desiring us to come up. They with the wings were instantly above through the hole. Only they with the ropes were in evil plight.

For as soon as ever one of us was up, he was commanded to draw up the ladder to him. At last each mans rope was hanged on an iron hook, so every one was fain to climb up by his rope as well as he could, which indeed was not compassed without blisters. Now as soon as we were all well up, the hole was again covered, and we were friendly received by the Virgin. This room was the whole breadth of the Tower itself having six very stately vestries a little raised above the room, and to be entered by the ascent of three steps. In these vestries we were distributed, there to pray for the life of the King and Queen. Meanwhile the Virgin went in and out of the little door, till we had done. For as soon as our process was absolved, there was brought in, and placed in the middle through the little door, by twelve person (which were formerly our musicians) a wonderful thing of a longish shape, which my companions took only to be a fountain. But I well observed that the corpse lay in it, for the inner chest was of an oval figure, so large that six persons might well lie in it one by another. After which they again went forth, fetched their instruments, and conducted in our Virgin, together with her she attendants, with a most delicate noise of music. The Virgin carried a little casket, but the rest only branches and small lamps, and some too lighted torches. The torches were immediately given into our hands, and we were to stand about the fountain in this order.

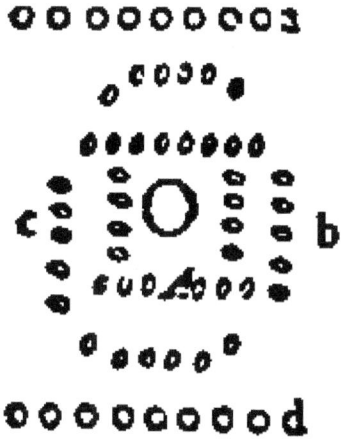

First stood the Virgin A with her attendants in a ring round about with the lamps and branches c. Next stood we with our torches b, then the musicians a in a long rank; last of all the rest of the virgins d in another long rank too. Now whence the virgins came, or whether they dwelt in the castle, or whether they were brought in by night, I know not, for all their faces were covered with delicate white linen, so that I could not know any of them. Hereupon the Virgin opened the casket, in which there was a round thing wrapped up in a piece green double taffeta. This she laid in the uppermost kettle, and then covered it with the lid, which was full of holes, and had besides a rim, on which she poured in some of the water which we had the day before prepared, whence the fountain began immediately to run, and through four small pipes to drive into the little kettle. Beneath the undermost kettle there were many sharp points, on which the virgins stuck their lamps, that so the heat might came to the kettle, and make the water seethe. Now the water beginning to simmer, by many little holes at a, it fell in upon the bodies, and was so hot, that it dissolved them all, and turned them into liquor.

But what the above said round wrapped up thing was, my companions knew not, but I understood that it was the Moor's head, from which the water conceived so great heat. At b round about the great kettle, there were again many holes, in which they stuck their branches. Now whether this was done of necessity, or only for ceremony, I know not. However, these branches were continually besprinkled by the fountain, whence it afterwards drops somewhat of a deeper yellow into the kettle. This lasted for near two hours, that the fountain still constantly ran of it self; but yet the longer, the fainter it was. Meantime the musicians went their way, and we walked up and down in the room, and truly the room was so made, that we had opportunity enough to pass away our time. There was, for images, paintings, clock-works, organs, springing fountains, and the like, nothing forgotten. Now it was near the time when the fountain ceased, and would run no longer, upon which the Virgin commanded a round golden globe to be brought. But at the bottom of the fountain there was a tap, by which she let out all the matter that was dissolved by those hot drops (whereof certain quarts were then very red) into the globe. The rest of the water which remained above in the kettle was poured out. And so this fountain (which was now become much lighter) was again carried forth. Now whether it was opened abroad, or whether anything of the bodies that was further useful yet remained, I dare not certainly say. But this I know, that the water that was emptied into the globe was much heavier than six or yet more of us were well able to bear, albeit for its bulk it should have seemed not too heavy for one man. Now this globe being with much ado gotten out of doors, we again sat alone, but I perceiving a trampling overhead, had an eye to my ladder. Hear one might take notice of the strange opinions my companions had concerning this fountain, for they not imagining but that the bodies lay in the garden of the castle, knew not what to make of this kind of working, but I thanked God that I awaked in so opportune a time, and saw that which helped me the better in all the Virgins business. After one quarter of an hour the cover above was again lifted off, and we commanded to come up, which was done as before with wings, ladders and ropes. And it did not a little vex me, that whereas the virgins could go up another way, we were fain to take so much toil; yet I could well judge there must be some special reason in it, and we must leave somewhat for the old man to do too. For even those with the wings had no advantage by them but when they were to mount through the hole. Now being gotten up thither also, and the hole shut again, I saw the globe hanging by a strong chain in the middle of the room. In this room was nothing else but mere windows, and still between two windows there was a door, which was covered with nothing but a great polished looking-glass; and these windows and looking-glasses were so optically opposed one to another, that although the sun (which now shined exceeding bright) beat only upon one door, yet (after the windows towards the sun were opened, and the doors before the looking-glasses drawn aside) in all quarters of the room there was nothing but suns, which by artificial refraction's beat upon the whole golden globe hanging in the midst, and for as much as the same (besides that brightness) was polished, it gave such a lustre, that none of us could open our eyes, but were therefore forced to look out at windows till the globe was well heated, and brought to the desired effect. Here I may well avow that in these mirrors I have seen the most wonderful spectacle that ever Nature brought to light, for there were suns in all places, and the globe in the middle shined yet brighter, so that but for one twinkling of an eye, we could no more endure it than the sun it self. At length the Virgin commanded to shut up the looking-glasses again, and to make fast the windows, and so let the globe cool again a little; and this was done about seven of the clock. Wherefore we thought good, since we might now have leisure a little to refresh our selves with a breakfast. This treatment was again right philosophical, and we had no need to be afraid of intemperance, yet we had no want. And the hope of the future joy (with which the Virgin continually comforted us) made us so jocund that we regarded not any pains, or inconvenience. And this I can truly say too concerning my companions of high quality, that their minds never ran after their kitchen or table, but their pleasure was only to attend upon this adventurous physic, and hence to contemplate the Creator's wisdom and omnipotency. After we had taken our refection, we again settled ourselves to work, for the globe was sufficiently cooled, which with toil and labour we were to lift off the chain and set upon the floor. Now the dispute was how to get the globe in sunder, for we were commanded to divide the same in the midst. The conclusion was that a sharp pointed diamond would best do it. Now when we had thus opened the globe, there was nothing of redness more to be seen, but a lovely great snow-white egg. It most mightily rejoiced us, that this was so well brought to pass. For the Virgin was in perpetual care, least the shell might still be too tender. We stood round about this egg as jocund as if we ourselves had laid it. But the Virgin made it presently be carried forth, and departed herself too from us again, and (as all ways) locked the door to. But what she did abroad with the egg, or whether it were some way privately handled, I know not, neither do I believe it. Yet we were again to pause together for one quarter of an hour, till the third hole were opened, and we by means of our instruments were come upon the fourth stone or floor. In this room we found a great copper kettle filled with yellow sand, which was warmed with a gentle fire. Afterwards the egg was raked up in it, that it might therein come to perfect maturity. This kettle was exactly square; upon one side stood these two verses, writ in great letters.

O. BLI. TO. BIT. MI. LI.
KANT. I. VOLT. BIT. TO. GOLT.
On the second side were these three words.
SANITAS. NIX. HASTA.
The third had no more but this one word.
F.I.A.T.

But on the hindermost part stood an entire inscription running thus.

QUOD
Ignis: Aer: Aqua: Terra:
SANCTIS REGUM ET REGINARUM NOSTR:
Cineribus
Eripere non potuerunt.
Fidelis Chymicorum Turba
IN HANC URNAM
Contulit.
A.D.

(What Fire: Air: Water: Earth Were unable to rob From the holy ashes OF OUR KINGS AND QUEENS Was gathered by our faithful flock of Achymists In this urn. A.D. 1459)

Now whether the sand or egg were hereby meant, I leave to the learned to dispute, yet do I my part, and omit nothing undeclared. Our egg being now ready was taken out, but it needed no cracking, for the bird that was in it soon freed himself, and showed himself very jocund, yet he looked very bloody and unshapen. We first set him upon the warm sand, so the Virgin commanded that before we gave him any thing to eat, we should be sure to make him fast, otherwise he would give us all work enough. This being done too, food was brought him, which surely was nothing else than the blood of the beheaded, diluted again with prepared water, by which the bird grew so fast under our eyes, that we well saw why the Virgin gave us such warning of him. He bit and scratched so devilishly about him, that could he have had his will upon any of us, he would soon have dispatched him. Now he was wholly black, and wild, wherefore other meat was brought him, perhaps the blood of another of the Royal Persons, whereupon all his black feathers moulted again, and instead of them there grew out snow-white feathers. He was somewhat tamer too, and suffered himself to be more tractable. Nevertheless we did not yet trust him. At the third feeding his feathers began to be so curiously coloured, that in all my life I never saw the like colours for beauty. He was also exceeding tame, and behaved himself so friendly with us, that (the Virgin consenting) we released him from his captivity. "Tis now reason," began our Virgin, "since by your diligence, and our old man's consent, the bird has attained both his life, and the highest perfection, that he be also joyfully consecrated by us." Herewith she commanded to bring dinner, and that we should again refresh ourselves, since the most troublesome part of our work was now over, and it was fit we should begin to enjoy our passed labours. We began to make ourselves merry together. Howbeit we had still all our mourning clothes on, which seemed somewhat reproachful to our mirth. Now the Virgin was perpetually inquisitive, perhaps to find to which of us her future purpose might prove serviceable. But her discourse was for the most part about Melting; and it pleased her well when one seemed expert in such compendious manuals as do peculiarly commend an artist. This dinner lasted not above three quarters of an hour, which we yet for the most part spent with our bird, whom we were fain constantly to feed with his meat, but he still continued much at the same growth. After dinner we were not long suffered to digest our meat, but after that the Virgin together with the bird was departed from us. The fifth room was set open to us, whither we got too after the former manner, and tendered our service. In this room a bath was prepared for our bird, which was so coloured with a fine white powder, that it had the appearance of mere milk. Now it was at first cool when the bird was set into it. He was mighty well pleased with it, drinking of it, and pleasantly sporting in it. But after it began to heat by reason of the lamps that were placed under it, we had enough to do to keep him in the bath. We therefore claps a cover on the kettle, and suffered him to thrust his head out through a hole, till he had in this sort lost all his feathers in this bath, and was as smooth as a newborn child, yet the heat did him no further harm, at which I much marvelled, for in this bath the feathers were quite consumed, and the bath was thereby tinged with blue. At length we gave the bird air, who of himself sprung out of the kettle, and was so glitteringly smooth, that it was a pleasure to behold it. But because he was still somewhat wild, we were fain to put a collar, with a chain, about his neck, and so led him up and down the room. Meantime a strong fire was made under the kettle, and the bath sodden away till it all came to a blue stone, which we took out, and having first pounded it, we were afterwards fain to grind it on a stone, and finally with this colour to paint the bird's whole skin over. Now he looks much more strangely, for he was all blue, except the head, which remained white. Herewith our work on this story was performed, and we (after the Virgin with her blue bird was departed from us) were called up through the hole to the sixth storey, where we were mightily troubled, for in the midst a little altar, every way like that in the King's hall above described, was placed. Upon which stood the six fore-mentioned particulars, and he himself (the bird) made the seventh. First of all the little fountain was set before him, out of which he drunk a good draught. Afterwards he pecked upon the white serpent until she bled mightily. This blood we were to receive into a golden cup, and pour it down the bird's throat, who was mighty averse from it. Then we dipped the serpents head in the fountain, upon which she again revived, and crept into her deaths head, so that I saw her no more for a long time after. Meantime the sphere turned constantly on, until it made the desired conjunction. Immediately the watch struck one, upon which there was a going another conjunction. Then the watch struck two. Finally, whilst we were observing the third conjunction, and the same was indicated by the watch, the poor bird of himself submissively laid down his neck upon the book, and willingly suffered his head (by one of us thereto chosen by lot) to be smitten off. Howbeit he yielded not one drop of blood, till he was opened on the breast, and then the blood spun out so fresh and clear as if it had been a fountain of rubies. His death went to the heart of us, and yet we might well judge that a naked bird would stand us in little stead. So we let it rest, and removed the little altar away and assisted the Virgin to burn the body (together with the little tablet hanging by) to ashes with fire kindled at the little taper; afterwards to cleanse the same several times, and to lay them in a box of cypress wood. Here I cannot conceal what a trick I and three more were served. After we had thus diligently taken up the ashes, the Virgin began to speak thus: "My lords, we are here in the sixth room, and have only one more before us, in which our trouble will be at an end, and then we shall return home again to our castle, to awaken our most gracious Lords and Ladies. Now albeit I could heartily wish that all of you, as you are here together, had behaved yourselves in such sort, that I might have given you commendations to our most renowned King and Queen, and you have obtained a suitable reward, yet because, contrary to my desire, I have found amongst you these four (herewith she pointed at me and three more) lazy and sluggish labourers, and yet according to my good-will to all and every one, am not willing to deliver them up to consign punishment; however, that such negligence may not remain wholly unpunished, I am purposed thus concerning them, that they shall only be excluded from the future seventh and most glorious action of all the rest, and so too they shall incur no further blame from their Royal Majesties." In what a case we now were at this speech I leave others to consider. For the Virgin so well knew how to keep her countenance, that the water soon ran over our basket; and we esteemed ourselves the most unhappy of all men. After this the Virgin by one of her maids (whereof there were many always at hand) caused the musicians to be fetched, who were with cornets to blow us out of doors with such scorn and derision that they themselves could hardly sound for laughing. But it did particularly mightily afflict us that the Virgin so vehemently laughed at our weeping, anger and impatience, and that there might well perhaps be some amongst our companions who were glad of this our misfortune. But it proved otherwise, for as soon as we were come out at the door, the musician bid us be of good cheer and follow them up the winding stairs. They led us up to the seventh floor under the roof, where we found the old man, whom we had not hitherto seen, standing upon a little round furnace. He received us friendly, and heartily congratulated us, that we were hereto chosen by the Virgin; but after he understood the affright we had conceived, his belly was ready to burst with laughing, that we had taken such good fortune so heinously. "Hence," said he, "my dear sons, learn that man never knoweth how well God intended him." During this discourse the Virgin also with her little box came running in, who (after she had sufficiently laughed at us) emptied her ashes into another vessel, and filled hers again with other matter, saying she must now go cast a mist before the other artists eyes, that we in the meantime should obey the old lord in whatsoever he commanded us, and not remit our former diligence. Herewith she departed from us into the seventh room whither she called our companions. Now what she first did with them there, I cannot tell, for they were not only most earnestly forbidden to speak of it, but we too by reason of our business, durst not peep on them through the ceiling. But this was our work. We were to moisten the ashes with our fore-prepared water till they became altogether like a very thin dough, after which we set the matter over the fire, till it was well heated. Then we cast it thus hot as it was into two little forms or moulds, and so let it cool a little (here we had leisure to look a while upon our companions through certain crevices made in the floor). They were now very busy at a furnace, and each was himself fain to blow up the fire with a pipe, and they stood thus blowing about it, as if they were herein wondrously preferred before us. And this blowing lasted so long till our old man roused us to our work again, so that I cannot say what was done afterwards. We having opened our little forms, there appeared two beautiful bright and almost transparent little images, the like to which mans eye never saw, a male and a female, each of them only four inches long and that which most mightily surprised me was that they were not hard, but limber and fleshy, as other human bodies, yet had they no life; so that I do most assuredly believe that the Lady Venus's image was also made after some such way. These angelically fair babes we first laid upon two little satin cushonets, and beheld them a good while, till we were almost besotted upon so exquisite an object. The old lord warned us to forbear, and continually to instil the blood of the bird (which had been received into a little golden cup) drop after drop into the mouths of the little images, from whence they apparently to the eye increased; and whereas they were before very small, they were now (according to proportion) much more beautiful, so that worthily all limners ought to have been here, and have been ashamed of their art in respect of these productions of nature. Now they began to grow so big that we lifted them from the little cushonets, and were fain to lay them upon a long table, which was covered with white velvet. The old man also commanded us to cover them over up to the breast with a piece of the fine white double taffeta, which because of their unspeakable beauty, almost went against us. But that I may be brief, before we had in this manner quite spent the blood, they were already in their perfect full growth. They had gold yellow curled hair, and the above mentioned figure of Venus was nothing to them. But there was not yet any natural warmth, or sensibility in them. They were dead figures, yet of a lively and natural colour, and since care was to be taken that they grew not too great, the old man would not permit any thing more to be given them, but quite covered their faces too with the silk, and caused the table to be stuck round about with torches. Here I must warn the reader that he imagine not these lights to have been of necessity, for the old man's intent hereby, was only that we should not observe when the soul entered into them, as indeed we should not have taken notice of it, in case I had not twice before seen the flames. However, I permitted the other three to remain in their belief, neither did the old man know that I had seen anything more. Hereupon he bid us sit down on a bench over against the table. Presently the Virgin came in too with the music and all furniture, and carried two curious white garments, the like to which I had never seen in the castle, neither can I describe them, for I thought no other than that they were mere crystal, but they were gentle, and not transparent, so that I cannot speak of them. These she laid down upon a table, and after she had disposed her virgins upon a bench round about, she and the old man began many legerdemain tricks about the table, which was done only to blind us. This (as I told you) was managed under the roof, which was wonderfully formed, for on the inside it was arched into seven hemispheres, of which the middlemost was somewhat the highest, and had at top a little round hole, which was nevertheless shut, and was observed by none else. After many ceremonies steps in six virgins, each of which bare a large trumpet, which were rouled about with a green glittering and burning material like a wreath, one of which the old man took, and after he had removed some of the lights at top, and uncovered their faces, he placed one of the trumpets upon the mouth of one of the bodies in such manner, that the upper and wider part of it was directed just against the fore-mentioned hole. Here my companions always looked upon the images, but I had other thoughts, for an soon as the foliage or wreath about the shank of the trumpet was kindled, I saw the hole at top open, and a bright stream of fire shooting down the tube, and passing into the body, whereupon the hole was again covered, and the trumpet removed. With this device my companions were deluded, so that they imagined that life came into the image by means of the fire of the foliage, for as soon as he received the soul he twinkled with his eyes, howbeit he scarce stirred. The second time he placed another tube upon its mouth, and kindled it again, and the soul was let down through the tube. This was repeated upon each of them three times, after which all the lights were extinguished and carried away. The velvet carpets of the table were cast together over them, and immediately a travelling bed was unlocked and made ready, into which thus wrapped up they were born, and so after the carpets were taken off them, they were neatly laid by each other, where with the curtains drawn before them, they slept a good while. (Now was it also time for the Virgin to see how our other artists behaved themselves. They were well pleased because, as the Virgin afterwards informed me, they were to work in gold, which is indeed a piece of this art, but not the most principal, most necessary and best. They had indeed too a part of these ashes, so that they imagined no other but that the whole bird was provided for the sake of gold, and that life must thereby be restored to the deceased.) Mean time we sat very still, attending when our married couple would awake. Thus about half an hour was spent. For then the wanton Cupid presented himself again, and after he had saluted us all, flew to them behind the curtain, tormenting them so long till they awaked. This happened to them with very great amazement, for they imagined no other but that they had hitherto slept from the very hour in which they were beheaded. Cupid, after he had awaked them, and renewed their acquaintance one with another, stepped aside a little, and permitted them both somewhat better to recruit themselves, mean time playing his tricks with us, and at length he would needs have the music fetched to be somewhat the merrier. Not long after the Virgin herself comes, and after she had most humbly saluted the young King and Queen (who found themselves somewhat faint) and kissed their hands, she brought them the two forementioned curious garments, which they put on, and so stepped forth. Now there were already prepared two very curious chairs, wherein they placed themselves, and so were by us with most profound reverence congratulated, for which the King in his own person most graciously returned his thanks, and again re-assured us of all grace. It was already about five of clock, wherefore they could make no longer stay, but as noon as ever the chiefest of their furniture could be laden, we were to attend the young Royal Persons down the winding stairs, through all doors and watches unto the ship, in which they embarked themselves, together with certain virgins and Cupid, and sailed so mighty swift that we soon lost sight of them, yet they were met (as I was informed) by certain stately ships. Thus in four hours time they had made many leagues out at sea. After five of clock the musicians were charged to carry all things back again to the ships, and to make themselves ready for the voyage. But because this was somewhat long a doing, the old lord commanded forth a party of his concealed soldiers, who had hitherto been planted in the wall, so that we had taken no notice of any of them, whereby I observed that this Tower was well provided against opposition. Now these soldiers made quick work with our stuff that no more remained further to be done but to go to supper. Now the table being completely furnished, the Virgin brings us again to our companions where we were to carry our selves as if we had truly been in a lamentable condition and forbear Laughing. But they were always smiling one upon another, howbeit some of them too sympathised with us. At this supper the old lord was with us too, who was a most sharp inspector over us, for none could propound any thing so discreetly, but that he knew how either to confute it, or amend it, or at least to give some good document upon it. I learned most by this lord, and it were very good that each one would apply himself to him, and take notice of his procedure, for then things would not so often and so untowardly miscarry. After we had taken our nocturnal reflection, the old lord led us into his closets of rarities, which were here and there dispersed amongst the bulwarks where we saw such wonderful productions of Nature, and other things too which man's wit in imitation of Nature had invented, that we needed a year more sufficiently to survey them. Thus we spent a good part of the night by candlelight. At last, because we were more inclined to sleep than see many rarities we were lodged in rooms in the wall, where we had not only costly good beds but also besides extraordinary handsome chambers, which made us the more wonder why we were the day before forced to undergo so many hardships. In this chamber I had good rest, and being for the most part without care, and weary with continual labour, the gentle rushing of the sea helped me to a sound and sweet sleep, for I continued in one dream from eleven of clock till eight in the morning.

THE SEVENTH DAY

After eight of clock I awaked, and quickly made myself ready, being desirous to return again into the Tower, but the dark passages in the wall were so many and various, that I wandred a good while before I could find the way out. The same happened to the rest too, till at last we all met again in the neither most vault, and habits entirely yellow were given us, together with our golden fleeces. At that time the Virgin declared to us that we were Knights of the Golden Stone, of which we were before ignorant. After we had now thus made ourselves ready, and taken our breakfast, the old man presented each of us with a medal of gold; on the one side stood these words,

AR. NAT. MI.
(*Ars Naturae Ministra*, Art is the priestess of nature)
On the other these,
TEM. NA. F.
(*Temporis Naturo Filia*, Nature is the daughter of time)

exhorting us moreover we should enterprise nothing beyond and against this token of remembrance. Herewith we went forth to the sea, where our ships lay so richly equipped, that it was not well possible but such brave things must first have been brought thither. The ships were twelve in number, six of ours, and six of the old lord's, who caused his ships to be freighted with well appointed soldiers. But he betook himself to us into our ship, where we all were together. In the first the musician seated themselves, of which the old lord had also a great number; they sailed before us to shorten the time. Our flags were the twelve celestial signs, and we sat in Libra. Besides other things our ship had also a noble and curious clock, which showed us all the minutes. The sea too was so calm, that it was a singular pleasure to sail. But that which surpassed all the rest, was the old man's discourse, who so well knew how to pass away our time with wonderful histories, that I could have been content to sail with him all my life long. Meantime the ships passed on amain, for before we had sailed two hours the mariner told us that he already knew the whole lake almost covered with ships, by which we could conjecture they were come out to meet us, which also proved true. For as soon as we were gotten out of the sea into the lake by the forementioned river, there presently stood in to us five hundred ships, one of which sparkled with mere gold and precious stones, in which sate the King and Queen, together with other lords, ladies, and virgins of high birth. As soon an they were well in ken of us the pieces were discharged on both sides, and there was such a din of trumpets, shalms, and kettle drums that all the ships upon the sea capered again. Finally, as soon as we came near they brought about our stripe together, and so made a stand. Immediately the old Atlas stepped forth on the King's behalf, asking a short, but handsome oration, wherein he welcomed us, and demanded whether the Royal Presents were in readiness. The rest of my companions were in an huge amazement, whence this. King should arise, for they imagined no other but that they must again awaken him. We suffered them to continue in their wonderment, and carried ourselves as if it seemed strange to us too. After Atlas's oration out steps our old man, making somewhat a larger reply, wherein he wished the King and Queen all happiness and increase, after which he delivered up a curious small casket, but what was in it, I know not, only it we committed to Cupid, who hovered between them both, to keep. After the oration was finished, they again let off a joyful voile of shot, and so we sailed on a good time together, till at length we arrived at another shore. This was near the first gate at which I first entered. At this place again there attended a great multitude of the King's family together with some hundreds of horses. Now as soon as we were come to shore, and disembarked, the King and Queen presented their hands to all of us one with another with singular kindness; and so we were to get up on horseback. Here I desire to have the reader friendly entreated not to interpret the following narration to any vain glory or pride of mine, but to credit me thus far, that if there had not been a special necessity in it, I could very well have utterly concealed this honour which was showed me. We were all one after another distributed amongst the lords. But our old lord, and I most unworthy, were to ride even with the King, each of us bearing a snow white ensign with a red cross. I indeed was made use of because of my age, for we both had long grey beards and hair. I had besides fastened my token round about my hat, of which the young King soon took notice, and demanded if I were he, who could at the gate redeem these tokens? I answered in most humble manner, Yea. But he laughed on me, saying, there henceforth needed no ceremony; I was HIS father. Then he asked me wherewith I had redeemed them? I replied, "With Water and Salt," whereupon he wondered who had made me so wise; upon which I grew somewhat more confident, and recounted unto him how it had happened to me with my bread, the Dove and the Raven, and he was pleased with it and said expressly that it must needs be, that God had herein vouchsafed me a singular happiness. Herewith we came to the first gate where the Porter with the blue clothes waited, who bore in his hand a supplication. Now as soon as he spied me even with the King, he delivered me the supplication, most humbly beseeching me to mention his ingenuity before the King. Now in the first place I demanded of the King, what the condition of this porter was? who friendly answered me, that he was a very famous and rare astrologer, and always in high regard with the Lord his Father, but having on a time committed a fault against Venus, and beheld her in her bed of rest, this punishment was therefore imposed upon him, that he should so long wait at the first gate, till some one should release him from thence. I replied, "May he then be released?" "Yes," said the King, "if any one can be found that hath as highly transgressed

as himself, he must stand in his stead, and the other shall be free."
This word went to my heart, for my conscience convinced me that
I was the offender, yet I held my peace, and herewith delivered
the supplication. As soon as he had read it, he was mightily
terrified, so that the Queen who, with our virgins, and that other
Queen besides, of whom I made mention at the hanging of the
weights, rid just behind us, observed it, and therefore asked him,
what this letter might signify. But he had no mind that he should
take notice of it, but putting up the paper, began to discourse of
other matters, till thus in about three hours time we came quite to
the castle, where we alighted, and waited upon the King into his
forementioned hall. Immediately the King called for the old Atlas
to come to him in a little closet, and showed him the writing, who
made no long tarrying, but rid out again to the Porter to take
better cognisance of the matter, after which the young King with
his spouse, and other lords, ladies and virgins sat down. Then
began our Virgin highly to commend the diligence we had used,
and the pains and labour we had undergone, requesting we might
be royally rewarded, and that she henceforward might be
permitted to enjoy the benefit of her commission. Then the old
lord stood up too, and attested that all that the Virgin had spoken
was true, and that it was but equity that we should both on both
parts be contented. Hereupon we were to step out a little, and it
was concluded that each man should make some possible wish,
and accordingly obtain it, for it was not to be doubted, but that
those of understanding would also make the best wish. So we
were to consider of it till after supper. Mean time the King and
Queen for recreations sake, began to fall to play together. It
looked not unlike chess, only it had other laws; for it was the
Virtues and Vices one against another, where it might ingeniously
be observed with what plots the Vices lay in wait for the Virtues,
and how to re-encounter them again. This was so properly and
artificially performed, that it were to be wished that we had the
like game too. During the game, in comes Atlas again, and asks
his report in private, yet I blushed all over, for my conscience gave
me no rest; after which the King gave me the supplication to read,
and contents whereof were much to this purpose. First he wished
the King prosperity, and increase; that his seed might be spread
abroad far and wide. Afterwards he remonstrated that the time
was now accomplished, wherein according to the royal promise he
ought to be released, because Venus was already uncovered by

one of his guests, for his observation could not lie to him. And that if his Majesty would please to make a strict and diligent enquiry, he would find that she had been uncovered, and in case this should not prove to be so, he would be content to remain before the gate all the days of his life. Then he sued in the most humble manner, that upon peril of body and life he might be permitted to be present at this nights supper. He was in good hopes to spy out the very offender, and obtain his wished freedom. This was expressly and handsomely indicted, by which I could well perceive his ingenuity, but it was too sharp for me, and I could well have endured never to have seen it. Now I was casting in my mind whether he might perchance be helped through my wish, so I asked the King, whether he might not be released some other way. "No," replied the King, "because there is a special consideration in the business. However, for this night, we may well gratify him in his desire." So he sent forth one to fetch him in. Meantime the tables were prepared in a spacious room, in which we had never been before, which was so complete, and in such manner contrived, that it is not possible for me only to begin to describe it. Into this we were conducted with singular pomp and ceremony. Cupid was not at this time present, for (as I was informed) the disgrace which had happened to his mother, had somewhat angered him. In brief, my offence, and the supplication which was delivered were an occasion of much sadness, for the King was in perplexity how to make inquisition amongst his guests, and the more because thus even they too, who were yet ignorant of the matter, would come to the knowledge of it. So he caused the Porter himself, who was already come, to make his strict surveigh, and showed himself as pleasant as he was able. Howbeit at length they began again to be merry, and to bespeak one another with all sorts of recreative and profitable discourses. Now how the treatment and other ceremonies were then performed, it is not necessary to declare, since it is neither the reader's concern, nor serviceable to my design. But all exceeded more in art, and human invention, than that we were overcharged with drinking. And this was the last, and noblest meal at which I was present. After the banquet the tables were suddenly taken away, and certain curious chairs placed round about in a circle, in which we together with the King and Queen, both their old men, the ladies and virgins, were to sit. After which a very handsome page opened the above-mentioned glorious little book, when

Atlas immediately placing himself in the midst, began to bespeak us to the ensuing purpose, that his Royal Majesty had not yet committed to oblivion the service we had done him, and how carefully we had attended our duty, and therefore by way of retribution had elected all and each of the Knights of the Golden Stone. That it was therefore further necessary not only once again to oblige ourselves towards his Royal Majesty, but to vow too upon the following articles, and then his Royal Majesty would likewise know how to behave himself towards his liege people. Upon which he caused the page to read over the articles, which were these.

I. You my lords the Knights, shall swear that you shall at no time ascribe your order either unto any devil or spirit, but only to God your Creator, and his hand-maid Nature.

II. That you will abominate all whoredom, incontinency and uncleanness, and not defile your order with such vices.

III. That you through your talents will be ready to assist all that are worthy, and have need of them.

IV. That you desire not to employ this honour to worldly pride and high authority.

V. That you shall not be willing to live longer than God will have you.

At this last article we could not choose but laugh sufficiently, and it may well have been placed after the rest, only for a conceit. Now being to vow to them all by the King's sceptre, we were afterwards with the usual ceremonies installed Knights, and amongst other privileges set over Ignorance, Poverty, and Sickness, to handle them at our pleasure. And this was afterwards ratified in a little chapel (whither we were conducted in all procession) and thanks returned to God for it, where I also at that time to the honour of God hung up my golden fleece and hat, and left them there for an eternal memorial. And because every one was there to write his name, I writ thus;

Summa Scientia nihil Scire,
Fr. CHRISTIANUS ROSENCREUTZ.
Eques aurei Lapidis.
Anno. 1459.

(The highest wisdom is to know nothing. Br(other) Christian Rosenkreutz. Knight of the Golden Stone A.D. 1459)

Others writ likewise, and truly each as seemed him good. After which we were again brought into the hall, where being sate down, we were admonished quickly to bethink ourselves what every one would wish. But the King and his party retired into a little closet, there to give audience to our wishes. Now each man was called in severally, so that I cannot speak of any man's proper wish. I thought nothing could be more praise-worthy than in honour of my order to demonstrate some laudable virtue, and found too that none at present could be more famous, and cost me more trouble than Gratitude. Wherefore not regarding that I might well have wished somewhat more dear and agreeable to my self, I vanquished my self, and concluded, even with my own peril, to free the Porter, my benefactor. Wherefore being now called in, I was first of all demanded whether, having read the supplication, I had observed or suspected nothing concerning the offender, upon which I began undauntedly to relate how all the business had passed. How through ignorance I fell into that mistake, and so offered myself to undergo all that I had thereby demerited. The King, and the rest of the lords wondered mightily at so unhoped for confession, and so wished me to step aside a little. Now as soon as I was called for in again, Atlas declared to me, that although it were grievous to the King's Majesty, that I whom he loved above others, was fallen into such a mischance, yet because it was not possible for him to transgress his ancient usages, he knew not how else to absolve me, but that the other must be at liberty, and I placed in his stead, yet he would hope that some other would be apprehended, that so I might be able to go home again. However, no release was to be hoped for, till the marriage feast of his future son. This sentence had near cost me my life, and I first hated myself and my twatling tongue, in that I could not hold my peace, yet at last I took courage, and because I considered there was no remedy, I related how this Porter had bestowed a token on me, and commended me to the other, by whose assistance I stood upon the scale, and so was made partaker of all the honour and joy already received. And therefore now it was but equal that I should shew my self grateful to my benefactor, and because the same could no way else be done, I returned thanks for the sentence, and was willing gladly to sustain some inconvenience for his sake, who had been helpful to me in coming to so high place. But if by my wish any thing might be effected, I wished my self at home again, and that so he by me, and I by my wish might be at liberty. Answer was made me, that the wishing stretched not so far. However I might well wish him free.

Yet it was very pleasing to his Royal Majesty that I had behaved my self so generously herein, but he was affraid I might still be ignorant into what a miserable condition I had plunged myself through this my curiosity. Hereupon the good man was pronounced free, and I with a sad heart was fain to step aside. After me the rest were called for too, who came jocundly out again, which was still more to my smart, for I imagined no other, but that I must finish my life under the gate. I had also many pensive thoughts running up and down in my head, what I should yet undertake, and wherewith to spend the time. At length I considered that I was now old, and according to the course of nature, had few years more to live. And that this anguish and melancholy life would easily dispatch me, and then my doorkeeping would be at an end, and that by a most happy sleep I might quickly bring myself into the grave. I had sundry of these thoughts. Sometimes it vexed me that I had seen such galant things, and must be robbed of them. Sometimes it rejoiced me that yet before my end I had been accepted to all joy, and should not be forced so shamefully to depart. This was the last and worst shock that I sustained. During these my cogitations the rest were ready. Wherefore after they had received a good night from the King and lords, each one was conducted into his lodging. But I most wretched man had nobody to show me the way, and yet must moreover suffer myself to be tormented, and that I might be certain of my future function, I was fain to put on the ring, which the other had before worn. Finally, the King exhorted me, that since this was now the last time I was like to see him in this manner, I should however behave myself according to my place, and not against the order. Upon which he took me also in his arms, and kissed me, all which I so understood as if in the morning I must sit at my gate. Now after they had all a while spoken friendly to me, and at last presented their hands, committing me to the divine protection, I was by both the old men, the Lord of the Tower. and Atlas, conducted into a glorious lodging, in which stood three beds, and each of us lay in one of them, where we yet spent almost two, &c.

Here are wanting about two leaves in quarto, and he (the author hereof), whereas he imagined he must in the morning be door keeper, returned home.

END

www.ingramcontent.com/pod-product-compliance
Lightning Source LLC
Chambersburg PA
CBHW071221160426
43196CB00012B/2366